Assessing Fish Predation on Migrating Juvenile Steelhead and a Retrospective Comparison to Steelhead Survival Through the Priest Rapids Hydroelectric Project, Columbia River, Washington, 2009–11

By Jill M. Hardiman, Timothy D. Counihan, U.S. Geological Survey; Dave S. Burgess, Katrina E. Simmons, Washington Department of Fish and Wildlife; Glen S. Holmberg, U.S. Geological Survey; Josh Rogala, and Rochelle Polacek, Washington Department of Fish and Wildlife

Prepared in cooperation with the Washington Department of Fish and Wildlife

Open File Report 2012–1129

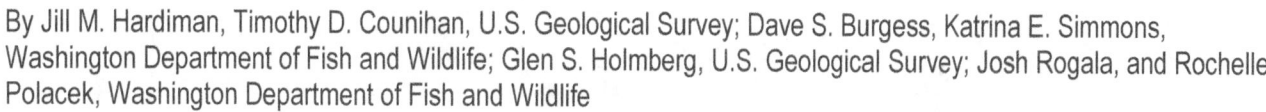

U.S. Department of the Interior
U.S. Geological Survey

U.S. Department of the Interior
KEN SALAZAR, Secretary

U.S. Geological Survey
Marcia K. McNutt, Director

U.S. Geological Survey, Reston, Virginia: 2012

For more information on the USGS—the Federal source for science about the Earth,
its natural and living resources, natural hazards, and the environment—visit
http://www.usgs.gov or call 1–888–ASK–USGS

For an overview of USGS information products, including maps, imagery, and publications,
visit http://www.usgs.gov/pubprod

To order this and other USGS information products, visit http://store.usgs.gov

Suggested citation:
Hardiman, J.M., Counihan, T.D., Burgess, D.S., Simmons, K.E., Holmberg, G., Rogala, J.A., and Polacek, R.R., 2012,
Assessing fish predation on migrating juvenile steelhead and a retrospective comparison to steelhead survival through
the Priest Rapids Hydroelectric Project, Columbia River, Washington, 2009–11: U.S. Geological Survey Open-File
Report 2012–1129, 36 p.

Contents

Figures

Conversion Factors and Abbreviations and Acronyms

Inch/Pound to SI

Multiply	By	To obtain
Length		
inch (in)	25.4	millimeter (mm)
foot (ft)	0.3048	meter (m)
mile (mi)	1.609	kilometer (km)
Area		
acre	0.4047	hectare (ha)
Flow rate		
Mass		
ounce, avoirdupois (oz)	28.35	gram (g)
pound, avoirdupois (lb)	0.4536	kilogram (kg)

Temperature in degrees Celsius (°C) may be converted to degrees Fahrenheit (°F) as follows: $°F=(1.8×°C)+32$

SI to Inch/Pound

Multiply	By	To obtain
Length		
millimeter (mm)	0.03937	inch (in.)
meter (m)	3.281	foot (ft)
kilometer (km)	0.62137	mile (mi)
Area		
hectare (ha)	2.47105	acre
square kilometer (km^2)	247.105	acre
Flow rate		
Mass		
gram (g)	0.03527	ounce, avoirdupois (oz)
kilogram (g)	2.20462	pound (lb)

Abbreviations and Acronyms

Abbreviation or Acronym	Meaning
BiOp	Biological Opinion
BRZ	Boat Restricted Zone
CPUE	Catch per unit effort
CRRL	Columbia River Research Laboratory
FERC	Federal Energy Regulatory Commission
GPS	Global Positioning System
GIS	Geographic Information System
NMFS	National Marine Fisheries Service
PRCC	Priest Rapids Coordinating Committee
RPAs	Reasonable and Prudent Alternatives
PRP	Priest Rapids Project
SOP	Standard Operating Procedures
USGS	United States Geological Survey
UTM	Universal Transverse Mercator
WDFW	Washington Department of Fish and Wildlife
USDA	U. S. Department of Agriculture
GRTS	Generalized Random Tessellation Stratified
GPP	Generator Powered Pulsator
PUD	Grant County Public Utility District Number 2
spp	species
RM	River mile
SE	Standard error

Assessing Fish Predation on Migrating Juvenile Steelhead and a Retrospective Comparison to Steelhead Survival Through the Priest Rapids Hydroelectric Project, Columbia River, Washington, 2009–11

By Jill M. Hardiman, Timothy D. Counihan, U.S. Geological Survey; Dave S. Burgess, Katrina E. Simmons, Washington Department of Fish and Wildlife; Glen S. Holmberg, U.S. Geological Survey; Josh Rogala, and Rochelle Polacek, Washington Department of Fish and Wildlife

Abstract

The U. S. Geological Survey (USGS) and the Washington Department of Fish and Wildlife (WDFW) have been working with the Public Utility District No. 2 of Grant County, Washington (Grant PUD), to increase their understanding of predator-prey interactions in the Priest Rapids Hydroelectric Project (PRP), Columbia River, Washington. For this study, the PRP is defined as the area approximately 6 kilometers upstream of Wanapum Dam to the Priest Rapids Dam tailrace, 397.1 miles from the mouth of the Columbia River. Past year's low survival numbers of juvenile steelhead (*Oncorhynchus mykiss*) through Wanapum and Priest Rapids Dams has prompted Grant PUD, on behalf of the Priest Rapids Coordinating Committee, to focus research efforts on steelhead migration and potential causal mechanisms for low survival. Steelhead passage survival in 2009 was estimated at 0.944 through the Wanapum Development (dam and reservoir) and 0.881 through the Priest Rapids Development and for 2010, steelhead survival was 0.855 for Wanapum Development and 0.904 for Priest Rapids Development. The USGS and WDFW implemented field collection efforts in 2011 for northern pikeminnow (*Ptychocheilus oregonensis*), smallmouth bass (*Micropterus dolomieu*), and walleye (*Sander vitreus*, formerly *Stizostedion vitreum*) and their diets in the PRP. For predator indexing, we collected 948 northern pikeminnow, 237 smallmouth bass, 18 walleye, and two largemouth bass (*Micropterus salmoides*). The intent of this study was to provide standardized predation indices within individual reaches of the PRP to discern spatial variability in predation patterns. Furthermore, the results of the 2011 study were compared to results of a concurrent steelhead survival study. Our results do not indicate excessively high predation of *Oncorhynchus* spp. occurring by northern pikeminnow or smallmouth bass in any particular reach throughout the study area. Although we found *Oncorhynchus* spp. in the predator diets, the relative proportion was small. Predation index values in 2011 were highest in the Priest Rapids mid-reservoir reach for northern pikeminnow and smallmouth bass. Predation indices generally were high in the tailrace areas for northern pikeminnow, and high in the forebay areas for smallmouth bass. Steelhead survival in 2011 was consistently high throughout the study period and the PRP, although predation indices were relatively low, which suggests that fish predation did not significantly affect steelhead survival throughout the study area. Our efforts to correlate retrospective predation indices with survival estimates for 2009 and 2010 did provide some evidence for high predation occurring in some of the same reaches, which had low steelhead survival, such as the Priest Rapids tailrace in 2009. However, for 2010, our results indicated that the loss of salmonids to predation were more contradictory to the survival results, where predation indices were higher for reaches in the Priest Rapids Development than in the Wanapum Development. Establishing correlations between steelhead survival and observed predation indices for previous research years, in 2009 and 2010 was confounded by the lack of coordination of these two studies during the initial study design, implementation period for such an analysis. Future efforts to correlate steelhead survival with fish predation would benefit from efforts to better coordinate the studies with consistent study reaches, and better timing of concurrent efforts.

Introduction

Anadromous juvenile salmonids (*Oncorhynchus* spp.) migrating through the Columbia River experience a variety of hazards that affect their survival as they migrate from freshwater rearing habitats to the ocean. Predation by native and non-native fish predators in the hydroelectric impoundments in the Columbia River has been an important factor in contributing to the total mortality of seaward migrating salmonids. The Public Utility District No. 2 of Grant County, Washington (Grant PUD), on behalf of the Priest Rapids Coordinating Committee (PRCC), has requested that the U. S. Geological Survey (USGS), Columbia River Research Laboratory, and Washington Department of Fish and Wildlife (WDFW) assist them in their efforts to evaluate the effects of native and introduced predatory fish on migrating juvenile salmon. During 2011, Grant PUD and the PRCC requested that we evaluate the effects of predation on migrating juvenile steelhead (*Oncorhynchus mykiss*) to provide insight into recently observed low survival of steelhead passing through the Priest Rapids Reservoir (Timko and others, 2010, 2011). Predation in the Lower Columbia River has been well documented as a significant factor affecting the survival of downstream-migrating salmonids (Poe and others, 1991; Vigg and others, 1991; Ward and others, 1995; Petersen and Ward, 1999). However, little work has been conducted in the Columbia River, upstream of the confluence with the Snake River, regarding predator effects. The USGS, in collaboration with the WDFW, has been working with the Grant PUD to conduct research using past studies from the Lower Columbia River and using technical advances in biological sciences to increase our understanding of predator-prey interactions in the Priest Rapids Hydroelectric Project (PRP). For this study, the PRP is defined as the area approximately 6 km upstream of Wanapum Dam to the Priest Rapids Dam tailrace, Columbia River, Washington.

In recent years, steelhead survival at Wanapum and Priest Rapids Dams has been below the Federal Energy Regulatory Commission performance standards for these dams. This became apparent, given the results of the "Behavior and Survival Analysis of Juvenile Steelhead and Sockeye Salmon through the Priest Rapids Hydroelectric Project" (hereafter referred to as "Steelhead Behavior and Survival Project") that was conducted by Blue Leaf Environmental, Inc., in 2009 and 2010 (Timko and others, 2010, 2011). The survival of juvenile steelhead migrating through the PRP was lower than the stipulated survival standards: juvenile steelhead passage survival of 95 percent at each dam, and 93 percent through a single development (one dam and reservoir; Federal Energy Regulatory Commission, 2008). Steelhead passage survival in 2009 was estimated at 0.9436 (standard error (SE)=0.0189) through the Wanapum Dam and reservoir and 0.8806 (SE=0.0206) for the Priest Rapids Dam and reservoir (Timko and others, 2010). Passage survival in 2010 was estimated at 0.8553 (SE=0.0186) for steelhead through the Wanapum Dam and reservoir while survival was higher at Priest Rapids Dam at 0.9037 (SE=0.0171; Timko and others, 2011). The performance standards (passage survival rates) were established for Grant PUD under the "Reasonable and Prudent Alternatives" (RPAs) in the National Marine Fisheries Service (NMFS) 2004 Biological Opinion (BiOp) for the Priest Rapids Project (National Marine Fisheries Service, 2004) and were adapted into the "Terms and Conditions" of the 2008 NMFS BiOp (National Marine Fisheries Service, 2008).

Given that the estimated steelhead survival does not conform to the established survival standards, the PRCC has shifted the focus of the "Steelhead Behavior and Survival Project" to assess the behavior and survival of steelhead through the Priest Rapids Dam and reservoir. Similarly, the PRCC has directed the USGS and WDFW to collaborate with Blue Leaf Environmental, Inc., to redirect USGS and WDFW efforts to focus on assessing the effects of piscivorous fish on steelhead in the Priest Rapids Dam and reservoir. Thus, foregoing any research at the Wanapum Dam and reservoir in 2011 (the final year of the Predator Indexing Project), our objectives were to relate the relative predation, as well as relative abundances of predators to survival estimates, generated by Blue Leaf Environmental, Inc., for tagged steelhead in the same study periods, reaches, and years.

Methods

Study Area

The 2011 study area consisted of the Priest Rapids Reservoir and approximately 6 km [3.7 river miles (RM)] upstream of Wanapum Dam in the Mid-Columbia River. Priest Rapids Reservoir is bounded by Wanapum Dam (RM 415) at the upstream extent, and Priest Rapids Dam (RM 397) at the downstream extent (fig. 1). The PRP consists of two run-of-the-river hydroelectric developments owned and operated by Grant PUD. The reservoir is approximately 18 mi long, with a shoreline of 56 mi, and an approximate surface area of 7,580 acres (Pfeifer and others, 2001). River environment conditions for the study area were collected from the Columbia River DART website (*http://www.cbr.washington.edu/dart/*).

Site Selection

In 2011, we focused our sampling effort in the Priest Rapids Reservoir and the Wanapum Dam forebay to evaluate predation effects of native and introduced predatory fish on juvenile salmonids as requested by the PRCC. The reservoir was divided into longitudinal sampling reaches consisting of:
    (1) Wanapum forebay,
    (2) Wanapum forebay near-Boat Restricted Zone (BRZ),
    (3) Wanapum forebay BRZ,
    (4) Wanapum tailrace BRZ,
    (5) Wanapum tailrace near-BRZ,
    (6) Wanapum tailrace,
    (7) Priest Rapids mid-reservoir,
    (8) Priest Rapids forebay,
    (9) Priest Rapids forebay near-BRZ, and
    (10) Priest Rapids forebay BRZ (fig. 1).
Reaches were developed to encompass ecologically significant habitat areas, such as hydrologic influence of the dam operations and potential predator distribution or behavioral differences, as well as sampling design issues such as accessibility and comparability with previous studies. Past studies have shown that predation of juvenile salmonids varies longitudinally in impoundments of the Columbia River (Petersen, 1994) and that areas very near hydroelectric dams, such as the BRZ areas, are where relatively high predation of juvenile salmonids occurs (Ward and others, 1995). We used a Geographic Information System (GIS) to further delineate habitat that was available for sampling by incorporating

bathymetry data and satellite imagery. Shoreline areas falling within the depth range of about 10 ft or less were delineated within the GIS for sampling by electrofishing. Sample site selection was performed using a sample frame developed with a Generalized Random Tessellation Stratified (GRTS) design (Larsen and others, 2007) with a point grid resolution of 30×30 m within the delineated shoreline areas. Individual sites were selected using this framework, such that sites were random and spatially balanced in each reach.

A sampling schedule was developed so that all reaches would be sampled throughout the reservoir within a 2 day block. This schedule excluded the BRZ areas that required dam operations to be altered during sampling efforts and were scheduled separately. In the 2011 study year, environmental conditions did not allow dam operations to be altered to allow for sampling in the BRZ areas. Four sample sites per sample outing were distributed among the longitudinal reaches so that no overlap would occur for individual electrofishing runs within a reach. In addition to the regularly sampled points, a list of alternate points were generated. The alternate sample points were used in the event that the regularly sampled points could not be sampled because of environmental conditions (for example low water conditions). For the forebay and tailrace reaches, the four points were allocated so that three sites were within the larger forebay (Priest Rapids and Wanapum) or tailrace (Wanapum) reach,with one point allocated to the near-BRZ reach. A number of additional sites were selected to be sampled repeatedly throughout the study period based on results from the 2010 study period that indicated either high predator abundance or predation. These sample points are referred to as "hotspots" for analysis. Once sites were selected, coordinates were entered into a marine GPS for navigating to sampling locations. Sampling week days were randomly assigned to reaches by sample week throughout the entire study period.

Fish Sampling

Electrofishing

We used standardized operating procedures for electrofishing (available upon request) to collect predators. All sampling equipment was calibrated prior to departing. Electrofishing was conducted at night using two 5.5 m Smith Root 5.0 Generator Powered Pulsator (GPP) electrofishing boats following WDFW warm-water sampling protocol (Bonar and others, 2000). Boat electrofishing began no earlier than one-half hour after sunset (determined using the Mattawa site from *http://www.usno.navy.mil/USNO/astronomical-applications/data-services/rs-one-year-us*). We operated individual electrofishing boats in a downstream direction parallel to the shoreline at a rate of 0.6–0.9 m/h, maintaining a distance from shore that allowed the inshore boom to fish entirely in the water, and avoiding areas that exceeded 10 ft in depth. Each site was electrofished for 600 s. Each crew consisted of one boat operator and two crew members that were outfitted with personal flotation devices, stationed at the front of the vessel, and equipped with 8-foot-long dipnets. To initiate fish galvanotaxis, we operated the GPP unit at approximately 1–2 amperes using a low power setting (50–500 volts) with a frequency between 30 and 120 Hz DC. Depending on water conductivity, we adjusted our pulse frequency and percentage of range as necessary. In addition, to prevent unnecessary fish injury, we noted the behavior of fish within the electrical field and adjusted the power accordingly to promote the galvanotaxis. The following information was recorded for each sample site: water temperature, specific conductance, time of day, transect start and end GPS coordinates, initials of crew, date, site designation, and power settings used to electrofish. During electrofishing, stunned fish were immediately placed into one of two onboard livewells equipped with a pump that continually added freshwater into the tank. After the completion of two sites, the boat was moored to shore, where staff collected the required biological information. In the event that transit time between sites was extended as a result of distance or environmental conditions, crews collected the pertinent data from the captured fish immediately after the completion of the first site.

Biological information was collected for the following target species: northern pikeminnow (*Ptychocheilus oregonensis*), smallmouth (*Micropterus dolomieu*) and largemouth bass (*Micropterus salmoides*), channel catfish (*Ictalurus punctatus*), and walleye (*Sander vitreus*, formerly *Stizostedion vitreum*), following standardized operating procedures (available upon request). Because of the potential for many of the captured fish to be consumed by anglers, under FDA guidelines it was not permissible to use the anesthetic commonly referred to as MS-222. Consequently, all fish captured were worked up in a non-anesthetized state. For all predatory fish (large- and smallmouth bass, walleye, and northern pikeminnow), diets and aging structures (scales, otoliths, and opercles) were collected, as well as total length, weight, sex, gonad maturity, and gonad weight where possible. The diets of walleye, smallmouth and largemouth bass, were collected using a lavage technique (non-lethal take) while northern pikeminnow and channel catfish stomachs were surgically removed (lethal take). All diets were preserved (either frozen whole, or contents soaked in 95-percent ethanol) and transported back to the laboratory to be analyzed for contents at a later date. In addition to the standard collections, we also performed a gross visual inspection of diets from collected predator stomachs at the request of PRCC members. The gross visual inspection was performed to assess the viability of rapid assessments in the field for salmonid predation. Non-predatory fish were worked up and released alive.

Because of a concurrent tagging and tracking project by Blue Leaf Environmental, Inc., in the Priest Rapids Development, all predatory fish were inspected for visual marks (dorsal hole punch or surgical scars) and scanned for PIT tags. Predatory fish that were tagged were worked up and released with minimal handling. Diet collection for these fish was accomplished by gastric lavage, and only scales were taken for aging. At the end of the work-up period, the boat operator and crew did quality-control checks on a randomly selected group of diets and aging structures collected from each site to ensure proper documentation.

Angling

In addition to boat electrofishing, northern pikeminnow were collected by U.S. Department of Agriculture (USDA) staff, angling from the transformer deck of Wanapum Dam tailrace. Angling was done during the night and we typically collected fish in the morning. To reduce the likelihood of using fish that had been dead for a long period of time with advanced stages of stomach content digestion, we communicated with angling crews to schedule times to pick up their captured fish. Upon arrival at the transformer deck, captured northern pikeminnow were immediately placed in individual bags in the event that stomach contents were expelled so they could then be associated with the specific predator. Once fish were bagged they were placed on ice, and were processed following the identical field and laboratory procedures used for predators captured by electrofishing.

Diet Analysis

Diet analysis was conducted in a laboratory setting using two different methodologies (SOPs available upon request)—one methodology for northern pikeminnow and another methodology for bass and walleye. The methodology for processing northern pikeminnow stomachs involved pancreatin digestion or maceration. Pancreatin digestion of northern pikeminnow gut contents works because a pikeminnow's stomach digests at a high pH leaving the mineral content of bones intact. Bass, walleye, and other piscivorous fish use acidic digestion, which demineralizes prey-fish bones leaving flaccid wisps that are completely dissolved by pancreatin. Therefore, bass and walleye diets were preserved in ethanol and analyzed separately from northern pikeminnow.

A major difference in the two methodologies is that prey fish are identified by diagnostic bones post pancreatin digestion for northern pikeminnow and therefore are not identifiable into more distinct categories (such as salmonid, non-salmonid) for pre-digestion prey weights. Northern pikeminnow diets were macerated with pancreatin and sodium sulfide nonahydrate between 40°C and 45°C. Pancreatin digests most tissue, but does not disintegrate or emulsify fat completely. A 1.5–2.0 molar solution of NaOH (lye) was therefore used to dissolve remaining fat. Samples were then rinsed through a 425-μm (#40) mesh sieve. The diagnostic bones we used to identify and enumerate fish (cleithra, dentaries, hyomandibular arches, pharyngeal arches, otoliths, and opercles) are paired structures on the left and right sides of fish. Therefore, bones were counted in pairs in order to avoid inflating the number of fish counted. For example, if we counted three left and two right salmon/steelhead cleithra of the same size, the total number of fish was recorded as three. For each individual northern pikeminnow diet that contained fish, the proportion of each prey fish count post-maceration was averaged to represent the mean percent composition of all diets analyzed.

Diet contents were separated into five categories: fish, crayfish, mollusks, insects, and miscellaneous (unidentifiable material and vegetation/inorganics) and weighed. The most common item in northern pikeminnow stomachs is the miscellaneous/unidentifiable category, consisting primarily of a mucilaginous substance that presumably is digesta and sloughed intestinal intima. Each prey category was compiled and weighed for each northern pikeminnow pre-maceration; after weighing, all diet items were returned to the sample bag to be macerated. Prey items in smallmouth bass and walleye diets were identified to the lowest practical taxon and blotted wet weights were recorded.

For each individual predator diet, the proportion of each prey item weight was averaged to represent the mean percent composition of all diets analyzed. Prey items were further identified within each prey category whenever possible. Prey fish categories included: Unknown fish species, Unknown salmonids, Unknown non-salmonids, Chinook (*Oncorhynchus tshawytscha*), Whitefish (*Coregonus* spp.), Salmon/Steelhead, Northern pikeminnow, Peamouth (*Mylcheilus caurinus*), Chiselmouth (*Acrocheilus alutaceus*), Redside shiner (*Richardsonius balteatus*), Dace spp., Cyprinid spp., *Cottus* spp., Threespine stickleback (*Gasterosteus aculeatus)*, Sucker spp., Walleye, *Lampetra* spp., Sand roller (*Percopsis transmontana*), and *Lepomis* spp. The unknown salmonid group consists of fish that could not be further identified and could include salmon, trout, char, or whitefish. The salmon/steelhead group includes fish in the genus *Oncorhynchus*. However, fish in that group cannot be identified beyond genus because their diagnostic bones are too similar. Chinook salmon were only identifiable because of the presence of coded wire tags or PIT tags. Zooplankton diet categories included: *Daphnia* spp., Bosminidae, Chydoridae, Copepoda, Ostracoda, and Sididae. Insect diet categories included: Insect parts, Diptera, Trichoptera, Lepidoptera, Ephemeroptera, Odonata, Orthoptera, Hemiptera, Hymenoptera, Coleoptera, Plecoptera, and unknown insects. Other diet items include: Amphipoda, Isopoda, Mollusca, Annelida, and Arachnida. For each individual predator diet that contained fish, the proportion of each prey fish was averaged to represent the mean percent composition of all diets analyzed.

Data Analyses

Relative Abundance Indices

We characterized the relative abundance of predatory fish by estimating the catch-per-unit effort (*CPUE*; number captured per 10 min) and by density and abundance indices (Burley and Poe, 1994). The *CPUE* was defined as the number of northern pikeminnow (total length greater than 170 mm), smallmouth bass (total length greater than 150 mm), and walleye (total length greater than 180 mm) captured during electrofishing efforts and then standardized to the number caught per 10 min. The abundance index (*AI*) was then estimated to be:

$$AI_i = DI_i \times S_i \quad (1)$$

where:

AI_i = Index of predator abundance in sampling area i,
DI_i = *CPUE* as the index of predator density in the sampling area i, and
S_i = Surface area (ha) for sampling area i, adjusted to include shoreline areas less than 10 ft in depth.

Estimates of S_i were derived using the GIS of the study area to estimate the area within each of the reaches sampled in 2011 that are less than 10 ft in depth.

Consumption Indices

Previous studies have demonstrated the analytical techniques we used to develop consumption indices for northern pikeminnow and smallmouth bass (Ward and others, 1995; Fritts and Pearsons, 2004). Ward and others (1995) based their consumption index on the concept of meal turnover-time (Windell, 1978; Rieman and others, 1991). We adopted the methods of Ward and others (1995) to estimate consumption of juvenile salmonids by northern pikeminnow collected within each reach. The consumption index (CI_{NPM}) used for northern pikeminnow was then:

$$CI_{NPM} = 0.0209 \cdot T^{1.60} \cdot W^{0.27} \cdot (n \cdot GW^{-0.61}) \quad (2)$$

where:

T = water temperature (°C),
W = predator weight (g),
GW = mean total gut weight (g), and
n = mean number of salmonids per northern pikeminnow.

We used the consumption index developed by Ward and Zimmerman (1999), who modified the relations developed by Rogers and Burley (1991) to describe smallmouth bass evacuation time as the consumption index for smallmouth bass (CI_{SMB}):

$$CI_{SMB} = 0.0407 \left(e^{0.15T} \cdot W^{0.23} \cdot \left(n \cdot GW^{-0.29} \right) \right) \quad (3)$$

7

where:

T = water temperature (°C),
W = predator weight (g),
GW = mean total gut weight (g), and
n = mean number of salmonids per smallmouth bass.

Predation Indices

We then combined the consumption indices with the abundance indices to calculate the predation index (Ward and others, 1995) as:

$$PI_i = AI_i \cdot CI_i \quad (4)$$

where:

PI_i = predation index for sample i,
AI_i = abundance index for area i, and
CI_i = consumption index for sample i.

Retrospective Steelhead Survival and Predation Analysis

An exploratory analysis was performed to compare survival estimates produced from acoustic-tagged steelhead to predation metrics generated by the USGS for concurrent time periods in 2009 and 2010. This exploratory analysis was requested after the PRCC received the steelhead survival estimates for 2009 and 2010 (Timko and others, 2010, 2011), which prompted concern over the survival estimates being lower than the stipulated standards for the PRP. This analysis was not planned at the time the studies were conducted, thus the analysis was performed after the low survival estimates were already reported. The low steelhead survival estimates prompted the PRCC to further pursue potential correlations (such as predation) with the survival results. The original USGS study that was designed during 2009 and 2010 was not formulated to coincide the sampling dates with the fish releases, or with the reaches used for survival estimation (Timko and others, 2010, 2011).

The retrospective analyses were based on data from study periods used in both the USGS efforts and those by Timko and others in 2009 and 2010 (Timko and others, 2010, 2011) to estimate steelhead survival. In 2009, the acoustic-tagged steelhead releases occurred from May 2 to June 7. In 2010, acoustic-tagged steelhead releases occurred from May 4 to June 2. Relative abundance, consumption, and predation indices were calculated for northern pikeminnow and smallmouth bass for the study periods that coincided (May 2–June 5, 2009; May 19–31, 2010) with the steelhead survival estimates generated by Timko and others (2010, 2011). Methodology for data collection for predator indexing in 2009 and 2010 for the USGS can be referenced in Counihan and others (2012), and for survival-estimation in the annual reports by Timko and others (2010, 2011). For these analyses, we matched the reaches we used to the reaches used by Timko and others (2010, 2011), for survival estimates for 2009 and 2010, as best as possible. However, the survival study reaches and predator-indexing reaches are not directly comparable. Furthermore, the USGS combined the near-BRZ forebay and tailrace with the larger forebay and tailrace reaches for study years 2010 and 2011 to better match the 2009 sample reaches as well as those used for survival estimation (Timko and others, 2010, 2011; Thompson and others, 2012). The mid-reservoir reaches between 2009 and the 2010 and 2011 study years were difficult to compare because the area available to sampling was expanded to cover the entire mid-reservoir area (all areas not defined as either forebay or tailrace) in the latter study years. In 2009, the Priest Rapids mid-reservoir reach consisted of a smaller area at approximately 3.7 mi (reach PM1) within the area defined as PM3 (fig. 1), which was used for the 2010 and 2011 study years.

Results

River Environment

Discharge in the 2011 study period was considerably higher than the 10-year average (83 percent higher from May 16 to July 18; Keeler, 2011), as well as those in the 2009 and 2010 study years (fig. 2). The elevated flows caused a high number of total dissolved-gas exceedance levels at Priest Rapids forebay, which were attributed to river flows in excess of Wanapum Dam's hydraulic capacity requiring involuntary spill (Keeler, 2011). Water temperatures in 2011 were lower than the 10-year average and the 2009 and 2010 study years (fig. 2).

Sampling Effort

High river flows and wind conditions prevented the predator index sampling from occurring as planned. The initial sampling schedule included 22 sampling days from May 10 to May 31. We were able to complete 11 sampling days in this time, and an additional 5 sample days from June 1 to June 9 (fig. 3). This encompassed the time period of tagged fish releases, but resulted in less frequent sampling than the daily fish releases. In order to accommodate for missed sampling trips, the study period was extended to June 9 to increase our predator collection efforts during the steelhead migration. In this time, 145 electrofishing runs within 8 of the 10 longitudinal reaches were completed. Sample efforts were originally planned to be allocated equally across reaches (forebay, mid-reservoir, and tailrace) with four efforts per outing (fig. 1). However, the sample efforts were not distributed across the reaches as planned throughout the study period because of adverse environmental conditions (fig. 4). The combined sample efforts for the four main study areas of Wanapum forebay, Wanapum tailrace, Priest Rapids mid-reservoir, and Priest Rapids forebay had similar weekly sample efforts, with the exception of the Wanapum tailrace (fig. 4). Wanapum tailrace was not sampled in the latter part of the study period. For the forebay areas, the near-BRZ reaches were sampled more frequently than prescribed in the study design in the latter half of the study period due to an emphasis on sampling in the prescribed "hotspot" sites in addition to the randomized sampling whenever WDFW was in this reach.

The study period for predator collection coincided with the juvenile salmon outmigration period for steelhead and other juvenile salmonids. Smolt passage data are not collected at Priest Rapids Dam, but our study period encompassed the peak period of the steelhead outmigration at Rock Island Dam (upstream from Wanapum Dam, fig. 5). Furthermore, our data collection efforts for the retrospective analysis for 2009 and 2010 also captured the peak steelhead migration (fig. 5) in those years.

Catch Data

We collected 5,313 fish comprising 23 species from the areas sampled in the 2011 predator indexing efforts. These results provide information about species composition during the study period, but are not a comprehensive list of fish species in the reservoir. For example, salmonids are avoided during electrofishing per our protocol, and non-target species are often counted and not netted. The most abundant fish captured were native catostomids (54.4 percent of total catch), primarily largescale sucker (37.7 percent of total catch), followed by northern pikeminnow (17.7 percent of total catch) (table 1). Non-native predators such as walleye and bass represented approximately 5 percent of the total catch. For predator indexing, we collected 948 northern pikeminnow from the study area. The total lengths of fish captured ranged from 38 to 532 mm; $\bar{x} = 180.5$ mm (fig. 6). We also collected 237 smallmouth bass, with total lengths ranging from 79 to 518 mm; $\bar{x} = 257.9$ mm (fig. 7). Other predators collected include 18 walleye with total lengths ranging from 192 to 728 mm; $\bar{x} = 490.1$ mm (fig. 8) and two largemouth bass with total lengths of 121 and 222 mm.

In addition to the predator indexing efforts, northern pikeminnow also were collected from the USDA staff, from angling efforts at the transformer deck of Wanapum Dam tailrace. A portion of these fish were set aside for WDFW staff for diet analysis. From these efforts, we collected 135 northern pikeminnow, with total lengths ranging from 135 to 582 mm; $\bar{x} = 456.9$ mm.

Relative Abundance Indices

The highest *CPUE* of northern pikeminnow (total length greater than 170 mm) occurred in the Priest Rapids mid-reservoir reaches in 2011, and was consistently high in 2009 and 2010 (table 2). The exception was in 2010 when the Priest Rapids tailrace (almost double the next highest *CPUE*) reach yielded the highest *CPUE* of all sampled reaches and years; however this reach was not sampled in 2011. For northern pikeminnow, the hotspot sampling sites resulted in similar *CPUE* results as the randomly selected sampling sites (table 2). For the retrospective analysis, an increasing catch trend was observed for northern pikeminnow from 2009 to 2011 in Priest Rapids forebay. Other *CPUE* results were relatively consistent across years for the Wanapum forebay and tailrace reaches for northern pikeminnow.

For smallmouth bass (total length greater than 150 mm), the *CPUE* was highest in the Priest Rapids forebay and mid-reservoir reaches, in 2011 (table 2). The hotspot analysis for smallmouth bass yielded higher *CPUE* results for the Priest Rapids forebay (0.049, SE=0.022) than the random sampling data (0.015, SE=0.003), but results from the two sampling designs were similar in other reaches. Trends were more difficult to detect across years for the retrospective analysis. One notable result was the consistently low *CPUE* in the tailrace reaches for smallmouth bass (range 0–0.005). In 2011, there were consistently more northern pikeminnow captured in the mid-reservoir and forebay areas than smallmouth bass (fig. 9). This may be a result of the greater relative abundance of northern pikeminnow than smallmouth bass.

Walleye were captured in just three reaches—Priest Rapids forebay, mid-reservoir, and Wanapum tailrace. This resulted in very low *CPUE* compared to the other piscivores (PF2, *CPUE* =0.001; PM3, *CPUE*=0.003, and WT2, *CPUE*=0.002). Of the 18 captured walleye, the majority were from Priest Rapids mid-reservoir (13 fish), with the remaining 5 captured walleye from the Priest Rapids forebay and the Wanapum tailrace.

Diet Analyses

Diet analyses was conducted on 561 northern pikeminnow collected via electrofishing and angling efforts (table 3). Fish were found in northern pikeminnow diets collected by electrofishing in the mid-reservoir and forebay of Priest Rapids Dam, and the forebay and tailrace of Wanapum Dam. Fish comprised 0.2–2.7 percent of the diets of northern pikeminnow from these reaches. The highest proportion of fish-prey items was in the Priest Rapids mid-reservoir (fig. 10). Of the 430 northern pikeminnow diets analyzed from electrofishing efforts, 13 (3 percent) of these fish contained salmon, consisting of a sum total of 17 identified salmonid prey items. Of the diets containing fish, the highest proportion containing salmonids occurred in the Priest Rapids forebay near-BRZ, followed by the Priest Rapids mid-reservoir, and the Wanapum tailrace reaches (fig. 11).

For northern pikeminnow collected by USDA anglers from the Wanapum Dam tailrace, fish comprised 18.9 percent of the diet. Of the 131 diets analyzed, 64 (49 percent) of these fish contained salmon, consisting of a sum total of 75 identified salmonid prey items. Prey items were identified by CWT and PIT tags as well as visual inspection and from diagnostic bones during laboratory analysis.

For the smallmouth bass, fish comprised a much higher proportion of the diet than for northern pikeminnow (fig. 12 and table 4). Of the 164 non-empty diets, 18 of these fish (11 percent) contained salmon, consisting of 21 total salmonid prey items. Smallmouth bass caught in the Wanapum forebay (WF1 and WF2 combined) had the highest proportion of salmonid prey based on proportion of all fish prey counts, followed by Priest Rapids mid-reservoir, and the Priest Rapids forebay (PF1 and PF2) (fig. 13). For walleye, fish comprised more than 97 percent of their diets. Of the 12 non-empty walleye diets, 11 of these contained salmonid prey items.

We determined that visual inspection alone was an unreliable method for salmon predation assessment. The results from the laboratory analysis consistently produced higher numbers of salmon prey than the field inspections (table 5). Laboratory analysis for steelhead identification generally was only confirmed by the presence of a PIT tag, and field identification was not reliable. This was evident by a steelhead that was recorded in the field, however, upon further laboratory analysis, the fish identified in the field was not a steelhead.

Predation Indices

For northern pikeminnow in our samples, predation of salmonids occurred in Priest Rapids forebay, mid-reservoir, and Wanapum tailrace reaches (table 6). The predation indices were consistently low across the reaches in 2011 for the randomized sampling, ranging from 0.068 to 1.191 (table 6), with Wanapum tailrace the highest ($P_i = 1.191$), followed by Priest Rapids mid-reservoir ($P_i = 0.595$). For the hotspot analysis, the predation indices ranged from 0 to 5.028, with predation only being documented in the the Priest Rapids near-BRZ forebay ($P_i = 0.035$) and the Priest Rapids mid-reservoir ($P_i = 5.028$). All other reaches were zero for the hotspot analysis. The predation index for the hotspots in Priest Rapids mid-reservoir was substantially higher than the randomly sampled sites within this reach. For the retrospective analysis, northern pikeminnow predation index values were high in Priest Rapids tailrace in 2009 and 2010 (table 7). Predation was not observed in the Priest Rapids mid-reservoir in the retrospective sampling window in 2009 and 2010, which contrasted with the relatively high index value for the 2011 analysis. No apparent trend could be distinguished across years for the Priest Rapids forebay and Wanapum tailrace and forebay reaches for northern pikeminnow.

Smallmouth bass predation occurred in the Priest Rapids forebay, forebay near-BRZ reach, the mid-reservoir, and Wanapum forebay near-BRZ reach. The predation index for the randomized sampling ranged from 0.039 to 1.827; the hotspot predation indices being very similar, ranged from 0.035 to 1.493 (table 6). The predation index for smallmouth bass was highest in Priest Rapids mid-reservoir, which was consistent with the northern pikeminnow results, followed by Wanapum forebay and the Priest Rapids forebay reaches. The hotspot analysis for smallmouth bass provided relatively consistent results to the randomized sites where predation occurred. For the retrospective analysis for smallmouth bass, the tailrace reaches were consistently zero across all years, and the Priest Rapids forebay predation indices were similar across years when predation occurred.

Discussion

We documented the relative predation of juvenile salmonids from the forebay of Priest Rapids Dam to the forebay of Wanapum Dam during the peak steelhead migration from 2009 to 2011. The intent of this research was to relate the relative predation, as well as relative abundances, of predators to survival estimates generated by Blueleaf Environmental, Inc., for tagged steelhead within the same study periods, reaches, and years. Environmental conditions in 2011 precluded us from sampling the study area concurrently with releases of tagged steelhead and confounded our interpretation of the relation of predation and survival. Furthermore, survival estimates in 2011, unlike those in 2010, were consistently high throughout the study area, suggesting there were few if any spatial differences and/or relationships between predator abundance, predation, and survival (Timko and others, 2011; Thompson and others, 2012). Additionally, our results did not indicate excessively high predation of *Oncorhynchus* spp. occurring by northern pikeminnow or smallmouth bass in any particular reach throughout the study area. We cannot infer direct causal mechanisms for the low steelhead survival estimates observed in the previous years because our studies were not specifically designed to address this question. For instance, the reaches that survival was estimated for during 2009 and 2010 (Timko and others, 2010, 2011) did not directly comport to the reaches we measured predation over. However, the fact that our results indicate relatively low predation in the study periods and reaches, low steelhead survival likely may have been caused by more than predation by northern pikeminnow and smallmouth bass alone. However, our exploratory work may help managers better understand where predator abundance and predation is high throughout the project.

During 2011, the predator index sampling efforts were confined to a relatively short time period (approximately 18 days) in which Thompson and others (2012) also were releasing tagged fish for survival estimation. The river environment during this time was such that on many occasions we could not safely conduct sampling in some reaches, so discerning temporal differences within or across reaches was not plausible. However, the extension of our sampling period past the release period of Thompson and others (2012) allowed for better coverage of the entire steelhead migration. This period coincided directly with the steelhead migration and should still capture peak predation events and provide insight to reaches where predator abundance and predation is high during the steelhead migration.

We observed spatial trends in relative abundance, consumption, and predation indices over the study period. As has been true in past evaluations of fish predation in the study area (Burley and Poe, 1994; Counihan and others, 2012), we observed the highest northern pikeminnow predation for the randomized sampling in one (WT2) of the two Wanapum Dam tailrace reaches we sampled during 2011. However, dissimilar to what was observed during 2009 and 2010, we observed higher predation in the Priest Rapids mid-reservoir reach than in the Wanapum tailrace reach. The highest predation index value for northern pikeminnow was from the 2011 Priest Rapids mid-reservoir hotspot sampling efforts, which focused on sites near the mouth of Crab Creek. Furthermore, when we combined the two Wanapum tailrace sections (WT1 and WT2) and examined the trends from 2010 to 2011, the northern pikeminnow predation in the Wanapum tailrace was less than that observed for the Priest Rapids mid-reservoir reach, and much less than that observed for the Wanpum tailrace during 2010. The relatively high discharge observed in 2011 may have altered the hydraulic environment in the tailrace areas to make them less suitable for northern pikeminnow while making conditions more favorable for predation events to occur in the mid-reservoir reach. Mesa and Olson (1993) determined the swimming performance of northern pikeminnow and reported that water velocities from 3.28 to 4.27 ft/s may reduce predation by northern pikeminnow around juvenile bypass outfalls at Columbia River dams. Thus, the high discharge during 2011 may have made areas in the Wanapum tailrace less favorable for northern pikeminnow, causing them to move downstream to the mid-reservoir reach. Futhermore, the result that predation was highest in the farthest downstream Wanapum tailrace reach (WT2) also indicates that pikeminnow may have been more prevalent in the downstream reaches.

For the smallmouth bass, we also observed spatial trends across the reaches for the predation indices. The predation indices generally were higher in the Priest Rapids mid-reservoir and the forebay reaches, relative to the tailrace reaches, and to the northern pikeminow results in these reaches. For smallmouth bass in the Priest Rapids forebay, the consumption indices were high in the near-BRZ reach (PF1). However, the predation index was lower for the near-BRZ reach than for the larger forebay reach (PF2)—this was driven by a lower abundance index. The highest predation impact for smolts will always be a combination of high abundance and high consumption occurring from predators. One interpretation of a reach with a high consumption index is that the habitat conditions of that reach are conducive to predation events and therefore could be considered a reach of concern for management. The near-BRZ reach is a likely surrogate for the BRZ reach, which could not be sampled due to environmental conditions precluding altering dam operations to allow for safe sampling of these reaches. Thus, our results are likely to be biased low due to the lack of sampling opportunity in the BRZ reaches. We know these reaches are likely a concern for high predator abundances and predation based on the results of our evaluations (Counihan and others, 2012) and other predator studies (Ward and others, 1995; Petersen and Ward, 1999). Other studies in the Columbia River basin have indicated differential predator abundance and predation based on longitudinal differences in reservoir areas, such as the forebay, tailrace, and mid-reservoir reaches (Beamesderfer and Rieman, 1991; Burley and Poe, 1994; Petersen, 1994). This is consistent with our results, and appears to be an interplay between capturing predation (consumption index) and abundance of predators. Furthermore, the tailrace environment also is an extremely difficult reach to sample with electrofishing gear, especially during the high discharges in 2011. Thus, there is the potential to underestimate predation in these areas.

Our results showing that northern pikeminnow and smallmouth bass predation were mostly low throughout the study area coupled with the reported high steelhead survival estimates through the Priest Rapids Reservoir (Thompson and others, 2012) suggest that fish predation was not a significant factor affecting steelhead survival during 2011. The estimates of steelhead survival from Thompson and others (2012) for 2011 indicate that survival was uniformly high with only two areas indicating survival probabilities that were much less than 1. Namely, these reaches included the Wanapum Dam forebay (release to RM 416, 0.9661, SE=0.0057) and Wanapum Dam and tailrace area (RM 416–413, 0.9816, SE=0.0046; Thompson and others, 2012). If fish predation were to have resulted in the mortality of steelhead in these areas, then we can infer from our data that smallmouth bass would have likely been the cause in the forebay area of Wanapum Dam and that northern pikeminnow would more likely to have been the cause in the tailrace, even though the geographic reaches in which our estimates encompass do not correspond directly to the survival reaches. For Wanapum Dam forebay, our reach WF2 is similar to the release to RM 416 of Thompson and others (2012), and our reaches WF1 and WT1 are similar to the RM 416–413 reach of Thompson and others (2012). The relatively low predation values we observed, and high survival observed by Thompson and others (2012) coupled with the presence of high discharges through the study area compared to 2009 and 2010 during the study period suggest that the high discharges may have promoted higher steelhead survival. Plumb and others (2006) documented relationships between flow and steelhead travel time and suggested that higher flows would result in higher steelhead survival.

Northern pikeminnow collected by USDA anglers from the Wanapum Dam tailrace contained a higher percentage of prey fish and salmon in their diets than fish collected from other areas. However, we were unable to effectively electrofish the areas being fished by the USDA anglers, although few existing fish-sampling gears would be effective in the Wanapum Dam tailrace environment during the salmonind migration period due to discharge conditions and dam operations. The northern pikeminnow captured here contained a higher proportion of juvenile salmonids; this does not seem surprising as few other prey items are likely to be available at this location. Further, it seems reasonable to assume that the sole reason for the northern pikeminnow to occupy this habitat at this time of the year would be to consume juvenile salmon (Ward and others, 1995). Gadomski and Hall-Griswold (1992) documented that northern pikeminnow preferentially consume dead or dying prey to live prey in a laboratory environment. The tailrace area of a hydroelectric project is where smolts are more likely to be disoriented, moribund, or dead and are likely found in higher concentrations in the tailrace area than the mid-reservoir reaches. The overall effect of northern pikeminnow occupying this habitat ultimately depends on the number of fish. If there are few fish, the effect will not be that great despite the fact that they consume proportionally higher numbers of juvenile salmonids; if there were many fish, then the effect would be greater. Effort could be expended to enumerate the northern pikeminnow in this location, but the fact that there are anglers actively trying to remove them from the river implies that their presence and effect is undesirable. Given this, identifying new and unique ways to remove them may be the best use of available financial resources versus spending a considerable amount of time estimating the population size of northern pikeminnow at this location. However, given that northern pikeminnow continue to be abundant in the study area, northern pikeminnow removed from this location are likely to be readily replaced.

The lack of a coordinated effort to simultaneously estimate survival and fish predation confounds our ability to retrospectively assess predation as a causal factor affecting the observed low steelhead survival through Priest Rapids Reservoir (Timko and others, 2010, 2011). During 2009 and 2010, survival estimates presented by Timko and others (2010, 2011) were presented for dam and reservoir, and some smaller reaches (for both Priest Rapids and Wanapum dams). Although the reaches over which they estimated survival do not match the reaches that we used to estimate predation during these years, we did see evidence of high predation by northern pikeminnow in the Priest Rapids tailrace during 2009, which also was indicated by Timko and others (2010) as an area with lower survival. In 2009, Timko and others (2010) also estimated that survival was lower downstream of the Wanapum Dam and Priest Rapids Dam tailrace reaches. Our results for this same period indicated that the predation was highest by northern pikeminnow in the Priest Rapids tailrace and by smallmouth bass in the Priest Rapids mid-reservoir reach. The fact that we did not see evidence of more predation occurring during this period could be confounded by the fact that we were capturing, tagging, and releasing some of the northern pikeminnow for a mark recapture study (Counihan and others, 2012) during 2009. Thus, it is plausible that some of the large northern pikeminnow that were released contained salmonids in their stomachs. However, this procedure was not continued in the 2010 and 2011 study years; during 2010, the highest predation index values were in the tailrace reaches of Wanapum and Priest Rapids Dams by northern pikeminnow, and in the Priest Rapids mid-reservoir by smallmouth bass. For northern pikeminnow, the predation index was more than four times higher in the Priest Rapids Dam tailrace versus the Wanapum Dam tailrace during 2010. However, the forebay reach of Wanapum Dam had a northern pikeminnow predation index of 0.251, while no predation was observed in the Priest Rapids forebay during this period. It is difficult to correlate the predation indices with the survival results for this area for the 2010 study period; the Priest Rapids Dam and reservoir survival (0.904, SE=0.017) was higher than Wanapum Dam and reservoir (0.855, SE= 0.019) survival estimates (Timko and others, 2011). If we assume predation is an indicator of low survival, our results indicate the potential for a high mortality of salmon in Priest Rapids tailrace. Predator movement between reaches also may confound correlations of survival to predation events if predators are consuming prey and then moving in between reaches. However, this is more likely to have occurred near the boundaries of reaches.

If efforts to relate survival estimates to fish predation are continued, we recommend continued efforts to coordinate studies examining survival and predation. Estimating the survival of juvenile salmonids and the predation of juvenile salmonids over the same reaches and time periods should provide insight into the effects of fish predators. Identifying problem areas for survival in past years, and following up with a study examining predation effects in those reaches at a later date, like the following year, may be of little utility due to the interaction between predator distributions and juvenile salmonid migration paths that may change with varying environmental conditions (such as high or low discharge years). Clearly, efforts to assess predation in years with high flows, such as 2011, is difficult. Thus, efforts to relate predation and survival would benefit from being conducted over multiple years. Further, limiting the scope to assess one particular juvenile salmonid species seems problematic as well, as the interaction between predators and prey will vary seasonally from year to year. We also caution trying to relate the survival of juvenile salmonids and predation over very short reaches such as those originally proposed (1 mi) and those eventually used by Thompson and others (2012) during 2011 (3 mi). The potential for bias in the estimates of survival from dead fish being transported through downstream arrays seems high and thus would bias associations with observed predation rates. Furthermore, there is an an increased potential for captured fish to move between small reaches and the associated predation values to be assigned to a different reach.

For future predation analyses, we recommend coverage of the peak salmon migration periods and sampling efforts throughout the reservoir, as well as a focused effort in areas with high potential for either predator abundance and/or predation. Our results for 2011, specifically the hotspot analysis, as well as those from Thompson and others (2012), indicate that the area near the mouth of Crab Creek (in the Priest Rapids mid-reservoir reach) is an area of potential concern. Efforts could be expended to continue to explore incorporating hotspots in conjunction with the randomized monitoring sample frame within the reservoir relative to survival and predation, specifically Crab Creek. We also recommend emphasis on other areas, such as the near-BRZ, and BRZ for both forebay and tailrace reaches. Furthermore, research efforts could be expended to to look into alternate predator collection and removal methods, to better understand the differences between angled fish and electrofishing collection results in the tailrace environments.

Acknowledgments

We thank Conrad Frost and Amy Puls of the USGS, and Curt Nelson, Fritz Wichterman, Klint Caillier, and seasonal and permanent staff of the WDFW for their assistance in the field and laboratory. We thank Lucinda Morrow and Lance Campbell of the WDFW aging laboratory. In addition, we thank Curt Dotson for contract administration and the members of the Priest Rapids Coordinating Committee for their comments and thoughts on this project. We also would like to acknowledge John Beeman and Matt Mesa, USGS, and Jeffrey Korth, WDFW, for their input and reviews of this report.

References Cited

Beamesderfer, R.C., and Rieman, B.E., 1991, Abundance and distribution of northern squawfish, walleyes and smallmouth bass in the John Day Reservoir, Columbia River: Transactions of the American Fisheries Society, v. 120, p. 439–447.

Bonar, S.A., Bolding, B.D., and Divens, M., 2000, Standard fish sampling guidelines for Washington state ponds and lakes: Washington Department of Fish and Wildlife Research Report FPT 00-28, Olympia, Wash.

Burley, C.C., and Poe, T.P., 1994, Significance of predation in the Columbia River from Priest Rapids Dam to Chief Joseph Dam: Prepared for Chelan, Douglas and Grant County Public Utility Districts by Washington Department of Wildlife and National Biological Survey, Olympia, Wash.

Counihan, T.D., Hardiman, J.M., Burgess, D.S., Simmons, K.E., Holmberg, G., Rogala, J.A., and Polacek, R.R., 2012 Assessing native and introduced fish predation on migrating juvenile salmon in Priest Rapids and Wanapum Reservoirs, Columbia River, Washington, 2009–11: U.S. Geological Survey Open-File Report 2012-1130, 68 p.

Fritts, A.L., and Pearsons, T.N., 2004, Smallmouth bass predation on hatchery and wild salmonids in the Yakima River, Washington: Transactions of the American Fisheries Society, v. 133, p. 880–895.

Federal Energy Regulatory Commission, 2008, Priest Rapids Project license agreement: Federal Energy Reglatory Commission, accessed June 1, 2012, at http://www.gcpud.org/pudDocuments/naturalResourcesDocs/h1.pdf.

Gadomski, D.M., and Hall-Griswold, J.A., 1992, Predation by Northern Squawfish on live and dead juvenile Chinook salmon: Transactions of the American Fisheries Society, v. 121, p. 680–685.

Keeler, C., 2011, Summary of 2011 annual fish-spill season and total dissolved gas monitoring: Prepared for Public Utility District No. 2 of Grant County, Ephrata, Wash.

Larsen, D.P., Olsen, A.R., Lanigan, S.H., Moyer, C., Jones, K.K., and Kincaid, T.M., 2007, Sound survey designs can facilitate integrating stream monitoring data across multiple programs: Journal of the American Water Resources Association, v. 43, p. 384–397.

Mesa, M.G., and Olson, T.M., 1993, Prolonged swimming performance of Northern Squawfish: Transactions of the American Fisheries Society, v. 122, no. 6, p. 1,104–1,110.

National Marine Fisheries Service, 2004, Biological opinion and Magnuson-Steven Fishery Conservation and Management Act—Interim Protection Plan for Operation of the Priest Rapids Hydroelectric Project, 115 p..

National Marine Fisheries Service, 2008, Biological Opinion and Magnuson-Steven Fishery Conservation and Management Act—New License for the Priest Rapids Hydroelectric Project, 74 p..

Petersen, J.H., 1994, Importance of spatial pattern in estimating predation on juvenile salmonids in the Columbia River: Transactions of the American Fisheries Society, v. 123, p. 924–930.

Petersen, J.H., and Ward, D.L., 1999, Development and corroboration of a bioenergetics model for northern pikeminnow feeding on juvenile salmonids in the Columbia River: Transactions of the American Fisheries Society, v. 128, p. 784–801.

Pfeifer, B., Hagen, J.E., Weitkamp, D., Bennett, D.H., Lukas, J., and Dresser, T., 2001, Evaluation of fish species present in the Priest Rapids Project area, Mid Columbia River, Washington, USA: Final Completion Report, Public Utility District No. 2 of Grant County, Ephrata, Wash.

Plumb, J.M., Perry, R.W., Adams, N.S., and Rondorf, D.W., 2006, The effects of river impoundment and hatchery rearing on the migration behavior of juvenile steelhead in the Lower Snake River, Washington: North American Journal of Fisheries Management, v. 26, no. 2, p. 438–452.

Poe, T.P., Hansel, H.C., Vigg, S., Palmer, D.E., and Prendergast, L.A., 1991, Feeding of predaceous fishes on out-migrating juvenile salmonids in John Day Reservoir, Columbia River: Transactions of the American Fisheries Society, v. 120, p. 405–420.

Rieman, B.E., Beamesderfer, R.C., Vigg, S., and Poe, T.P., 1991, Estimated loss of juvenile salmonids to predation by northern squawfish, walleyes, and smallmouth bass in John Day Reservoir, Columbia River: Transactions of the American Fisheries Society, v. 120, p. 448–458.

Rogers, J.B., and Burley, C.C., 1991, A sigmoid model to predict gastric evacuation rates of smallmouth bass (*Micropterus dolomieui*) fed juvenile salmon: Canadian Journal of Fisheries and Aquatic Sciences, v. 48, p. 933–937.

Thompson, A.M., O'Connor, R.R., Timko, M.A., Sullivan, L.S., Rizor, S.E., Hannity, J.L., Wright, C.D., Fitzgerald, C.A., Meagher, M.L., Stephenson, J.D., Skalski, J.R., and Townsend, R.L., 2012, Evaluation of downstream juvenile steelhead survival and predator-prey interacations using JSATS through the Priest Rapids Reservoir in 2011: Final Report submitted to Grant County Public Utility District No. 2 of Grant County, Wash.

Timko, M.A., Sullivan, L.S., Wright, C.D., Rizor, S.E., O'Connor, R.R., Fitzgerald, C.A., Meagher, M.L., Kikes, T.J., Stephanson, J.D., Skalski, J.R., and Townsend, R.L., 2010, Behavior and survival analysis of steelhead and sockeye through the Priest Rapids Hydroelectric project in 2009: Final Report submitted to Grant County Public Utility District No. 2 of Grant County, Wash.

Timko, M.A., Sullivan, L.S., O'Connor, R.R., Wright, C.D., Rizor, S.E., Hannity, J.L., Fitzgerald, C.A., Meagher, M.L., Stephenson, J.D., Skalski, J.R., and Townsend, R.L., 2011, Behavior and survival analysis of juvenile steelhead and sockeye salmon through the Priest Rapids Hydroelectric project in 2010: Draft Report submitted to Grant County Public Utility District No. 2, Grant County, Wash.

Vigg, S., Poe, T.P., Prendergast, L.A., and Hansel, H.C., 1991, Rates of consumption of juvenile salmonids and alternative prey fish by northern squawfish, walleyes, smallmouth bass, and channel catfish in John Day Reservoir, Columbia River: Transactions of the American Fisheries Society, v. 120, p. 421–438.

Ward, D. L., Petersen, J.H., and Loch, J.J., 1995, Index of predation on juvenile salmonids by northern squawfish in the Lower and Middle Columbia River and in the Lower Snake River: Transacations of the American Fisheries Society, v. 124, p. 321–324.

Ward, D.L., and Zimmerman, M.P., 1999, Response of smallmouth bass to sustained removals of northern pikeminnow in the lower Columbia and Snake Rivers: Transactions of the American Fisheries Society, v. 128, no. 6, p. 1,020–1,035.

Windell, J.T., 1978, Estimating food consumption rates of fish populations, *in* Bagenal, T., ed., Methods for assessment of fish production in fresh waters: London, Blackwell Scientific Publications, p. 227–254.

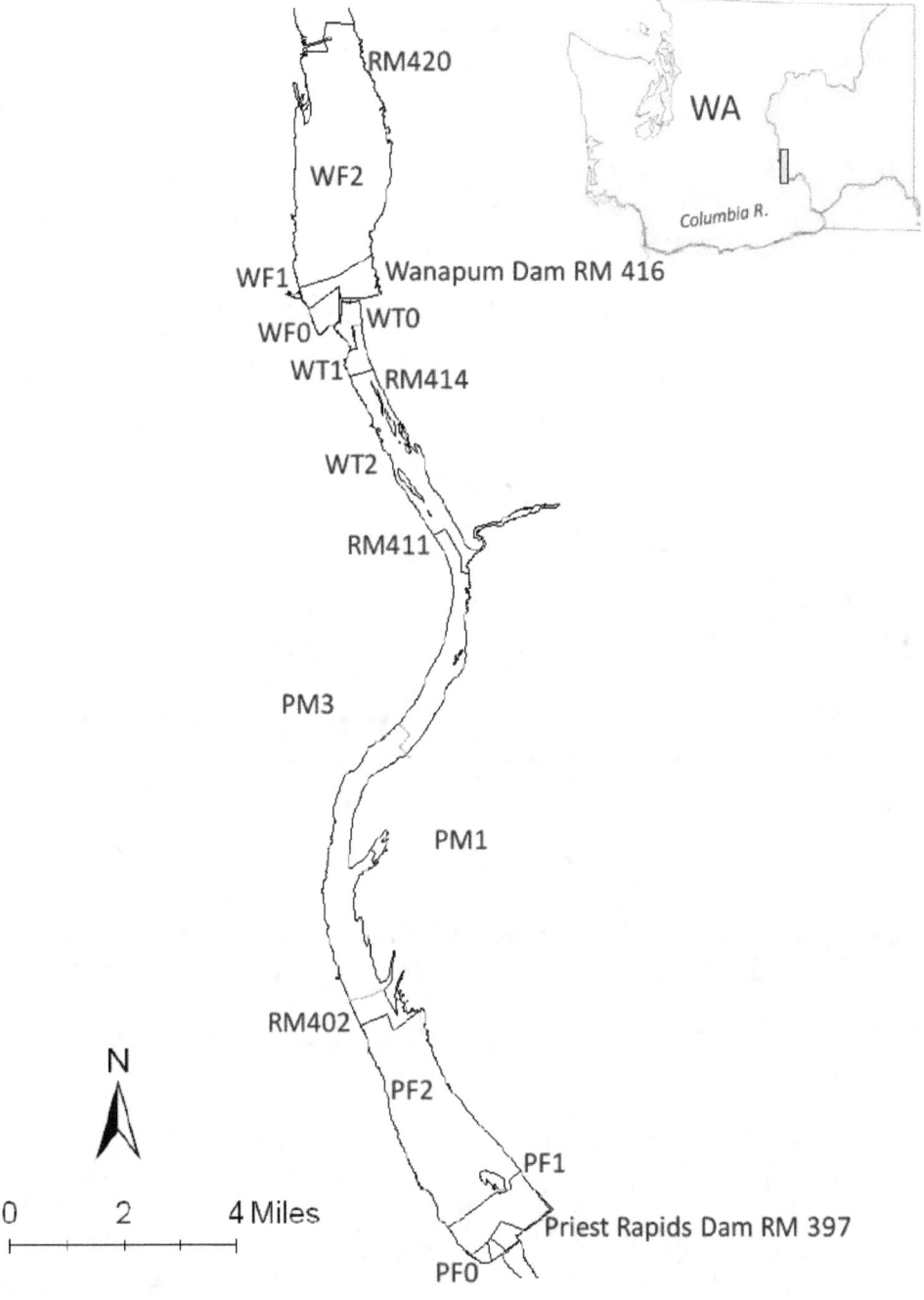

Figure 1. Study area depicting Priest Rapids Hydroelectric Project from upstream of Wanapum Dam to Priest Rapids Dam, Columbia River, Washington. Study reaches are delineated and defined as: WF2, Wanapum forebay; WF1, Wanapum forebay near-BRZ (Boat Restricted Zone); WF0, Wanapum forebay BRZ; WT0, Wanapum tailrace BRZ; WT1, Wanapum tailrace near-BRZ; WT2, Wanapum tailrace; PM3, Priest Rapids mid-reservoir (study years 2010 and 2011); PM1, Priest Rapids mid-reservoir (study year 2009; delineated by gray line); PF2, Priest Rapids forebay; PF1, Priest Rapids forebay near-BRZ; PF0, Priest Rapids forebay BRZ.

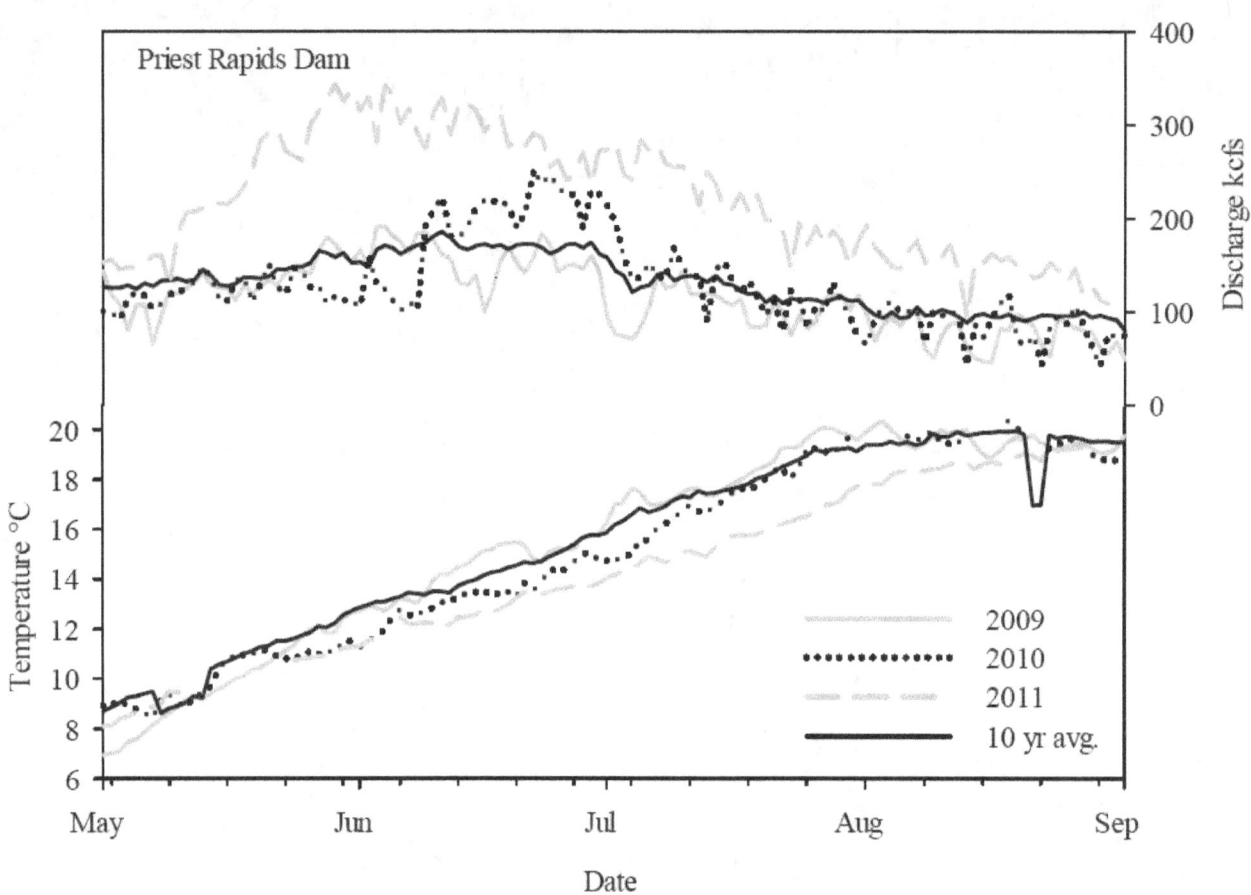

Figure 2. River conditions, discharge, and temperature in degrees Celsius (°C) at Priest Rapids Dam, Columbia River, Washington, from May to August, 2011 (dashed line), 2010 (dotted line), 2009 (gray line), and the 10-year average (solid line).

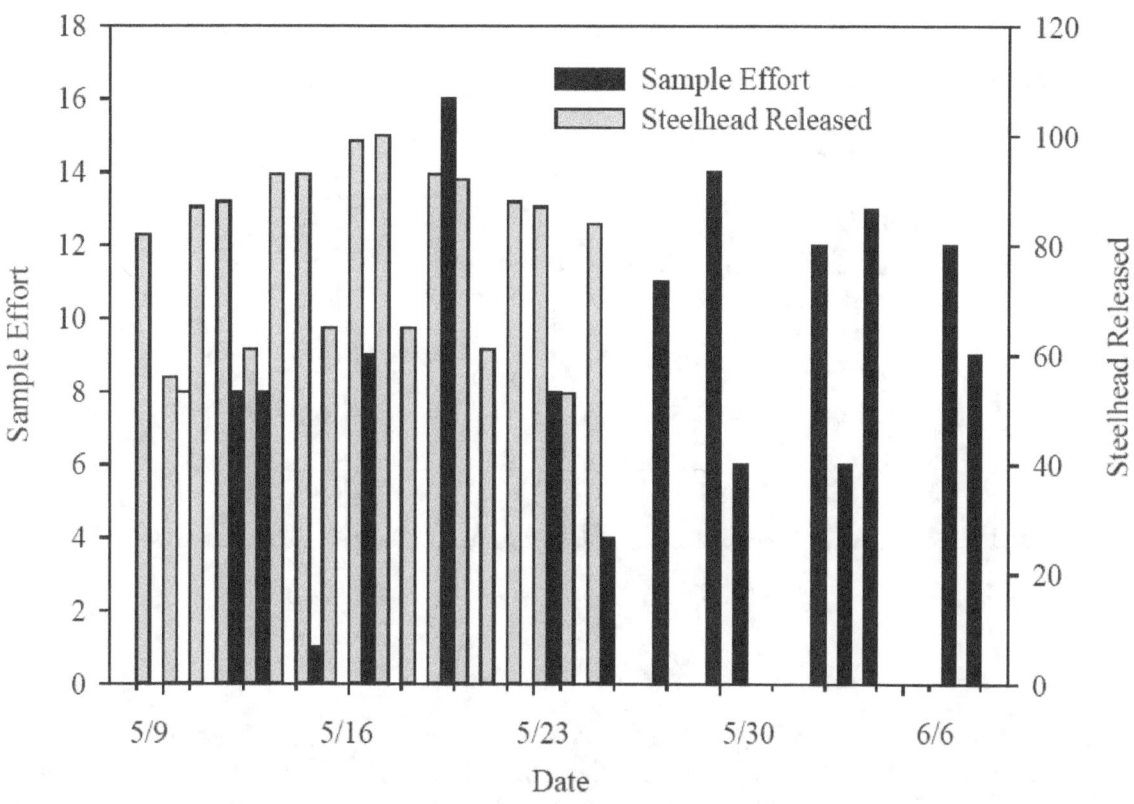

Figure 3. Summary of sample effort (number of electrofishing runs) for a predator indexing study by Washington Department of Fish and Wildlife, and the number of acoustic-tagged juvenile steelhead released for a concurrent survival study from May 8 to June 10, 2011, Priest Rapids Project, Columbia River, Washington.

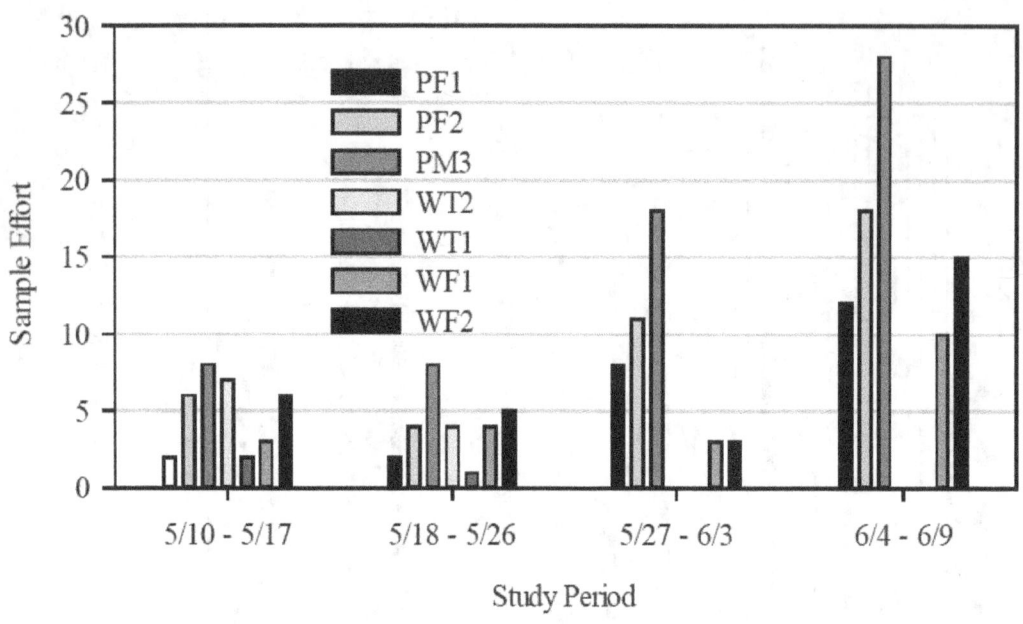

Figure 4. Distribution of sample effort (number of electrofishing runs) completed across the reaches, May 10–June 9, 2011, Priest Rapids Project, Columbia River, Washington. Reach locations: PF1, Priest Rapids forebay near-BRZ (Boat Restricted Zone); PF2, Priest Rapids forebay; PM3, Priest Rapids mid-reservoir; WT2, Wanapum tailrace; WT1, Wanapum tailrace near-BRZ; WF1, Wanapum forebay near-BRZ; WF2, Wanapum forebay.

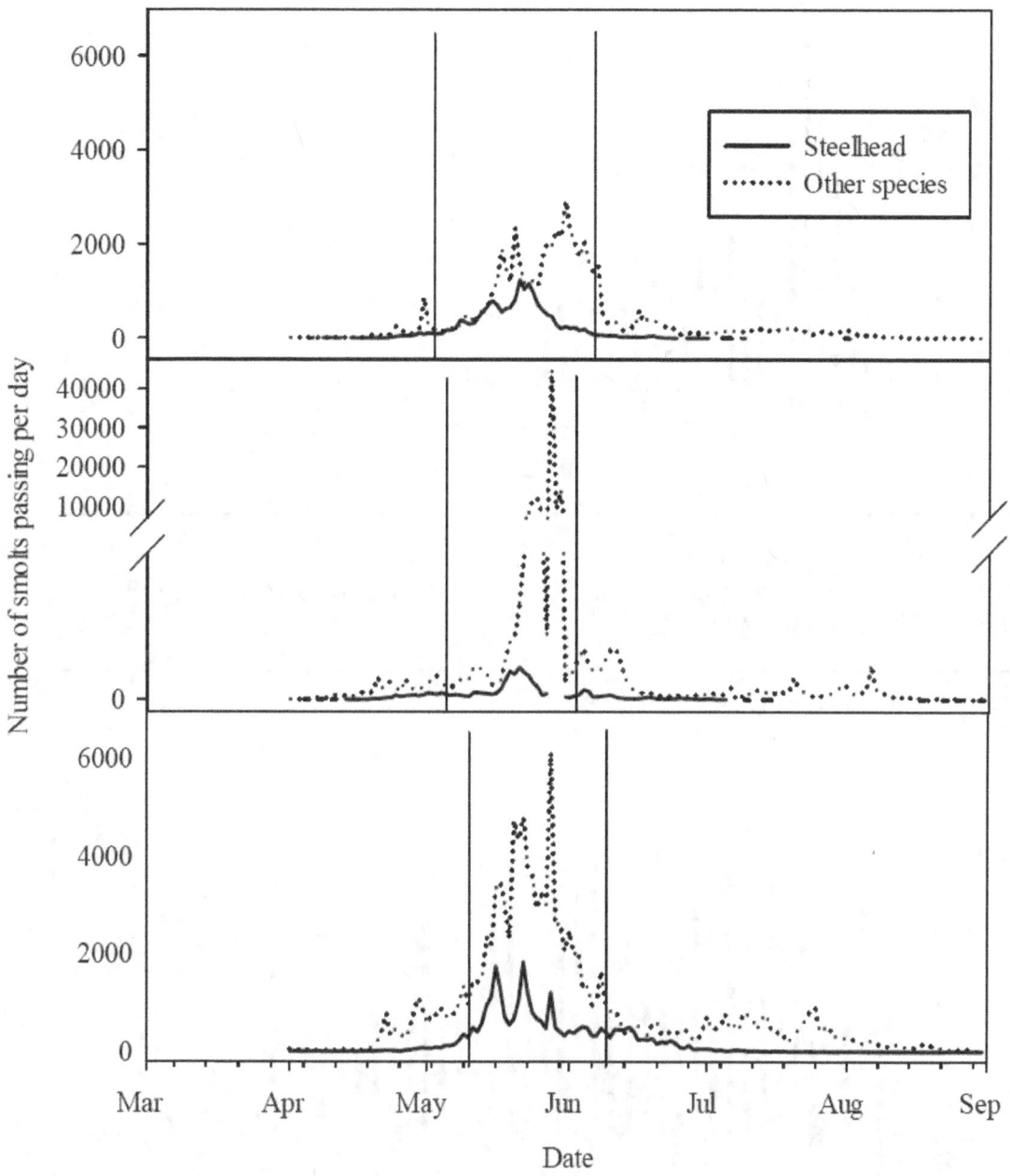

Figure 5. Daily juvenile salmonid downstream passage counts at Rock Island Dam, Columbia River, Washington, in 2009 (top), 2010 (middle), and 2011 (bottom), showing predator data-collection periods with vertical straight lines. Daily steelhead (solid line) counts include all rearing types (wild, hatchery, and unknown), and other species include Chinook-0, Chinook-1, coho, and sockeye. Data are from the Fish Passage Center Columbia River Dart website (*http://www.cbr.washington.edu/dart/*).

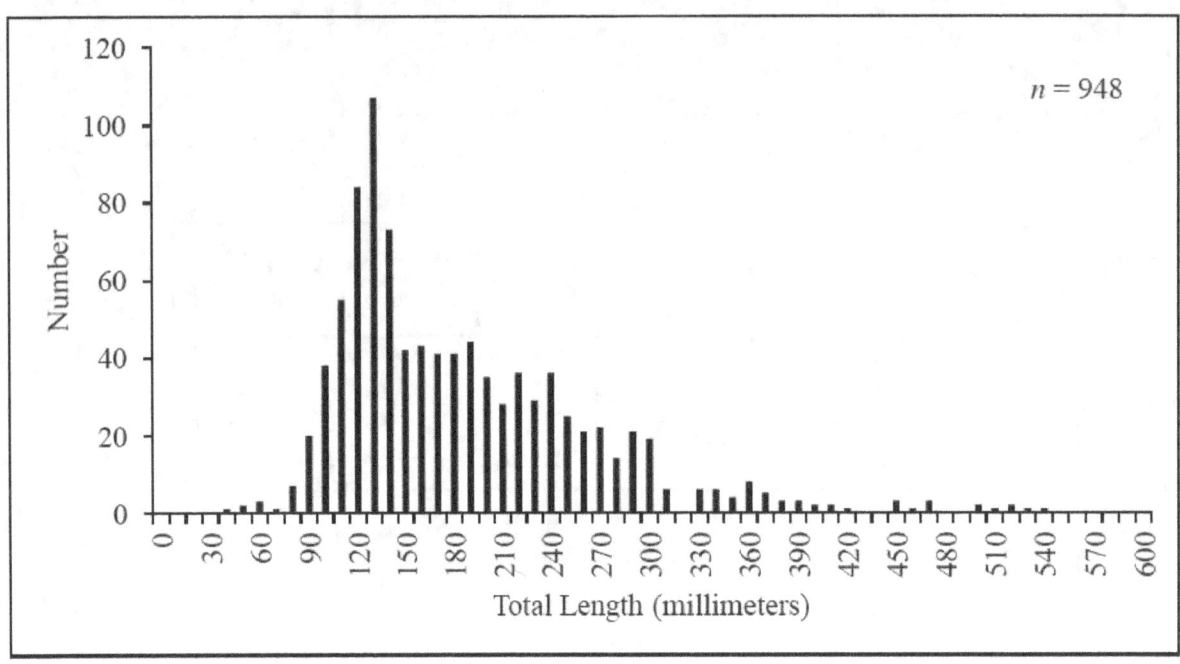

Figure 6. Total lengths of northern pikeminnow captured during electrofishing efforts, May 10–June 9, 2011, Priest Rapids Project, Columbia River, Washington.

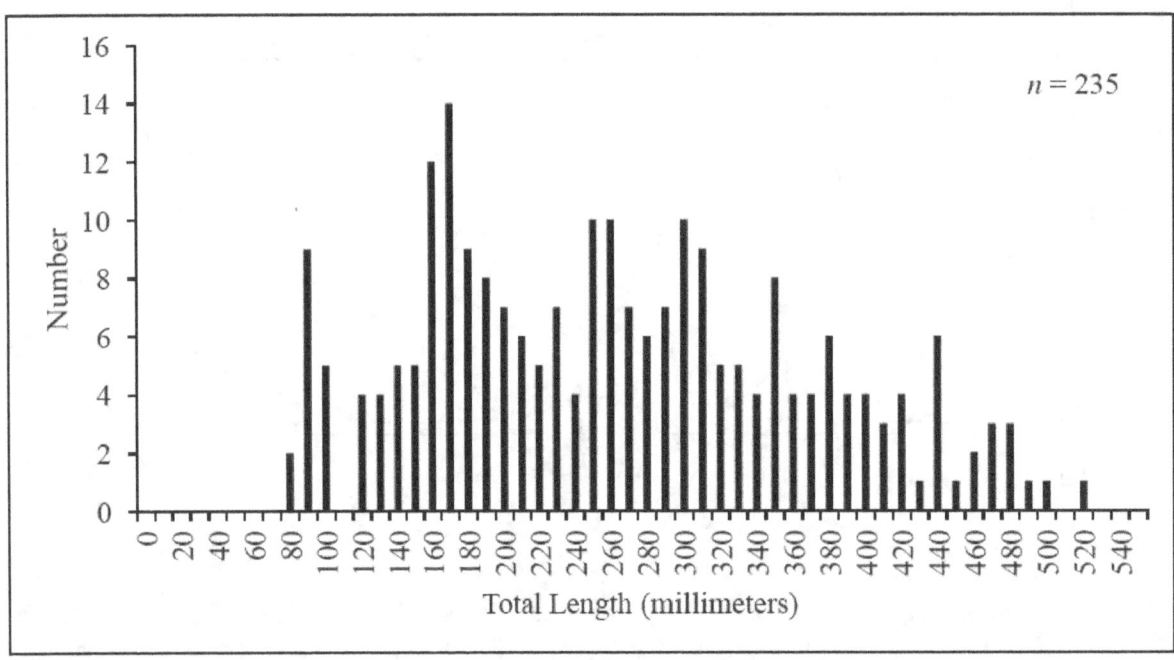

Figure 7. Total lengths of smallmouth bass captured during electrofishing efforts, May 10–June 9, 2011, Priest Rapids Project, Columbia River, Washington.

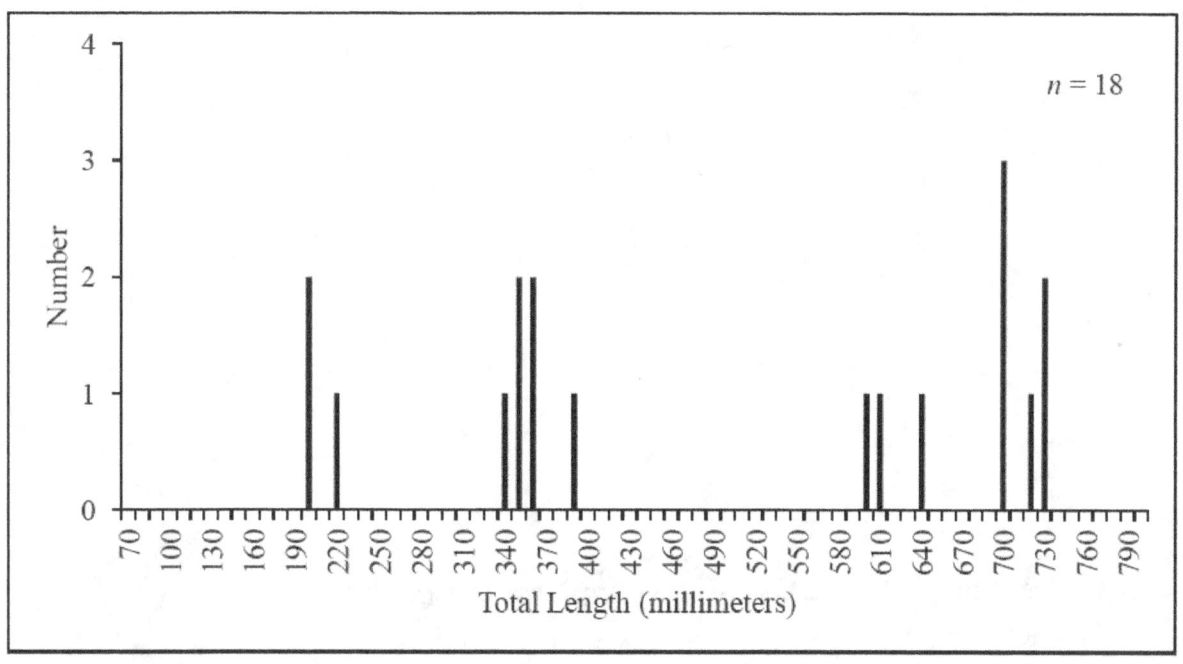

Figure 8. Total lengths of walleye captured during electrofishing efforts, May 10–June 9, 2011, Priest Rapids Project, Columbia River, Washington.

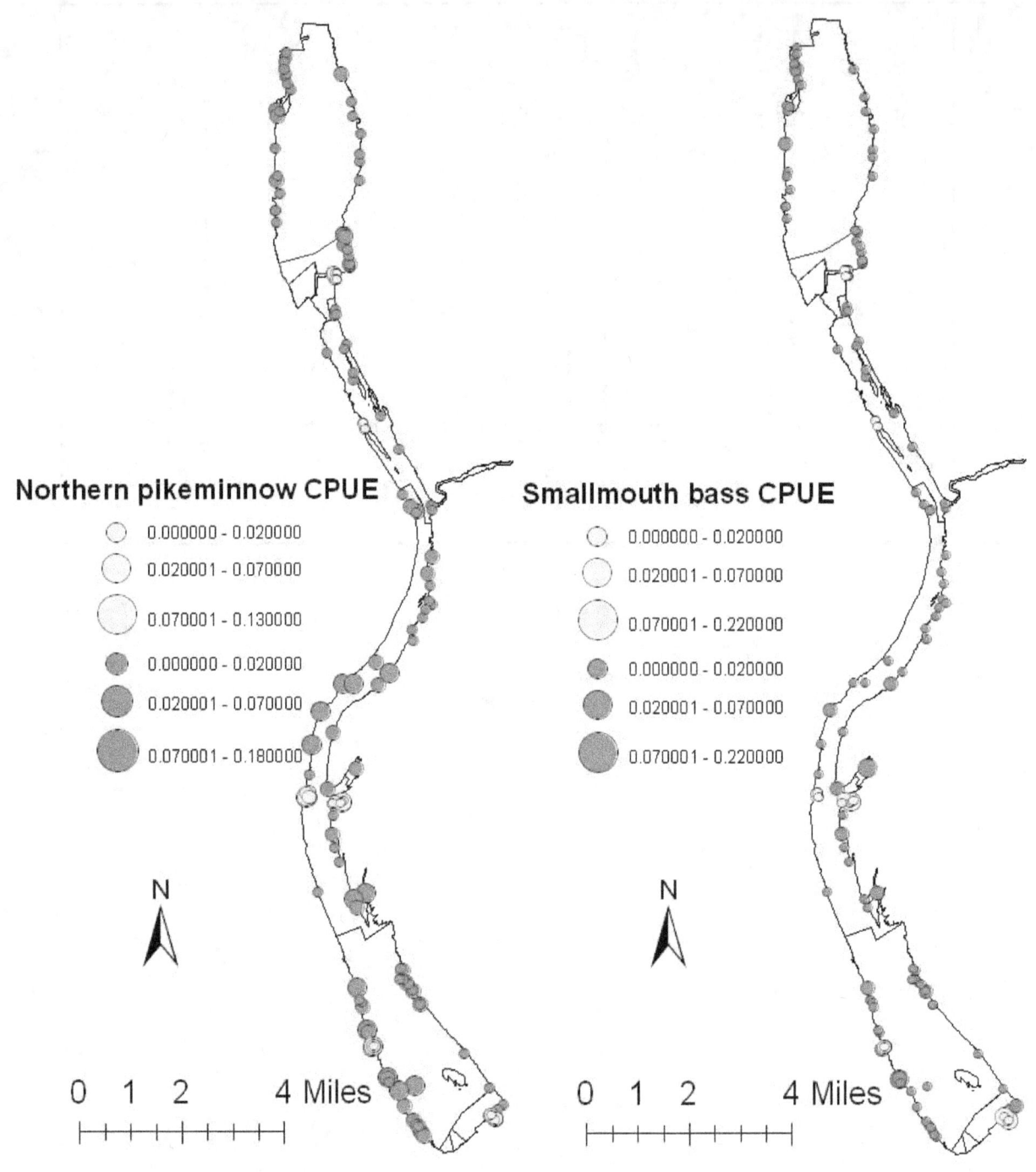

Figure 9. Spatial representation of catch per unit effort (number of fish caught per 10 minutes of boat electrofishing; *CPUE*) for northern pikeminnow (total length greater than 170 mm) and smallmouth bass (total length greater than 150 mm) during May 10 to June 9, 2011, at the Priest Rapids Hydroelectric Project, Columbia River, Washington. The yellow symbols indicate sample sites were part of a "hotspot" sample frame, and orange sites were part of a randomized sample frame.

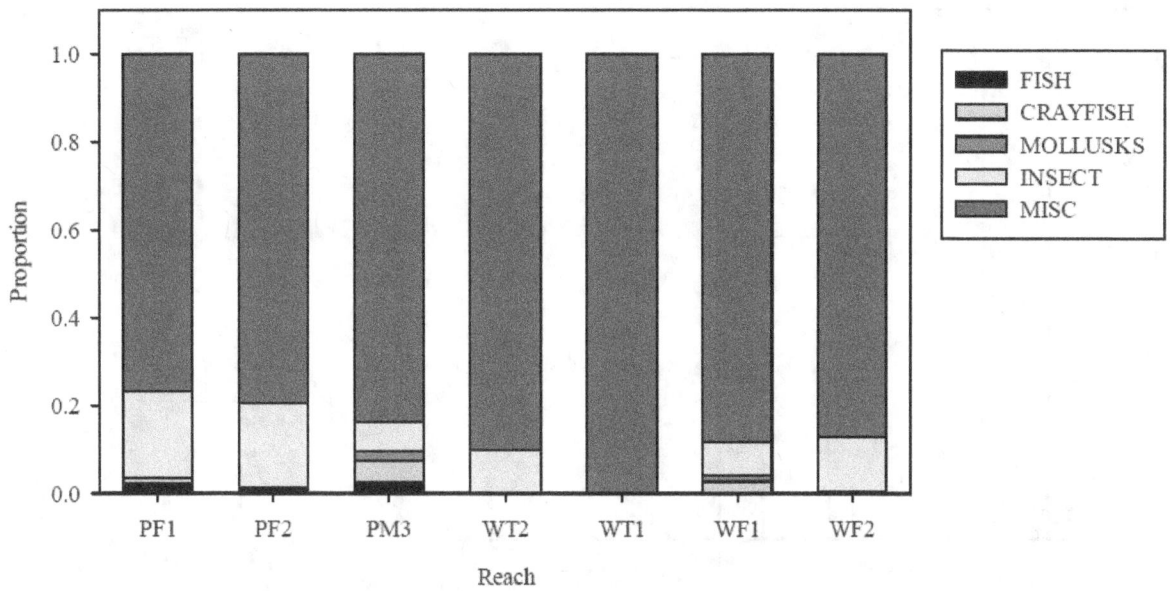

Figure 10. Diet composition by weight of northern pikeminnow in 2011 (May 10–June 9), by reach in the Priest Rapids Project, Columbia River, Washington. Reaches with no column indicate no diet sample. Reach locations: PF1, Priest Rapids forebay near-BRZ (Boat Restricted Zone); PF2, Priest Rapids forebay; PM3, Priest Rapids mid-reservoir; WT2, Wanapum tailrace; WT1, Wanapum tailrace near-BRZ; WF1, Wanapum forebay near-BRZ; WF2, Wanapum forebay.

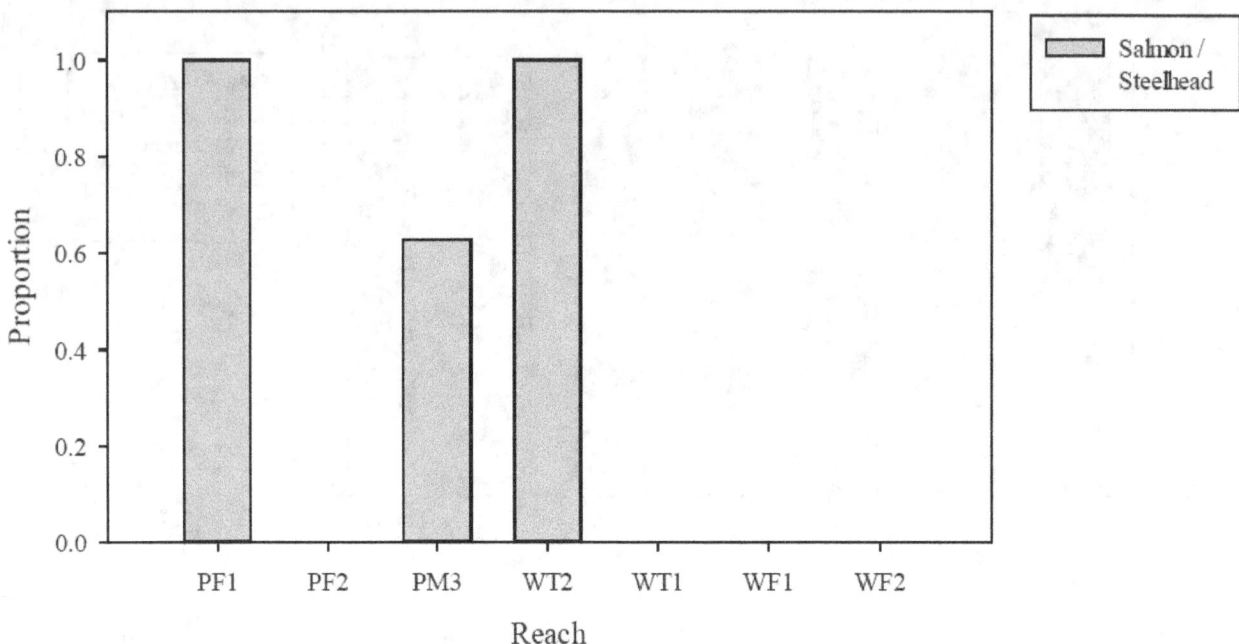

Figure 11. Proportion of fish in diet that are salmon and steelhead for northern pikeminnow by reach during sampling in 2011 (May 10–June 9) in the Priest Rapids Project, Columbia River, Washington. Reaches with no column indicate no diet sample. Reach locations: PF1, Priest Rapids forebay near-BRZ (Boat Restricted Zone); PF2, Priest Rapids forebay; PM3, Priest Rapids mid-reservoir; WT2, Wanapum tailrace; WT1, Wanapum tailrace near-BRZ; WF1, Wanapum forebay near-BRZ; WF2, Wanapum forebay.

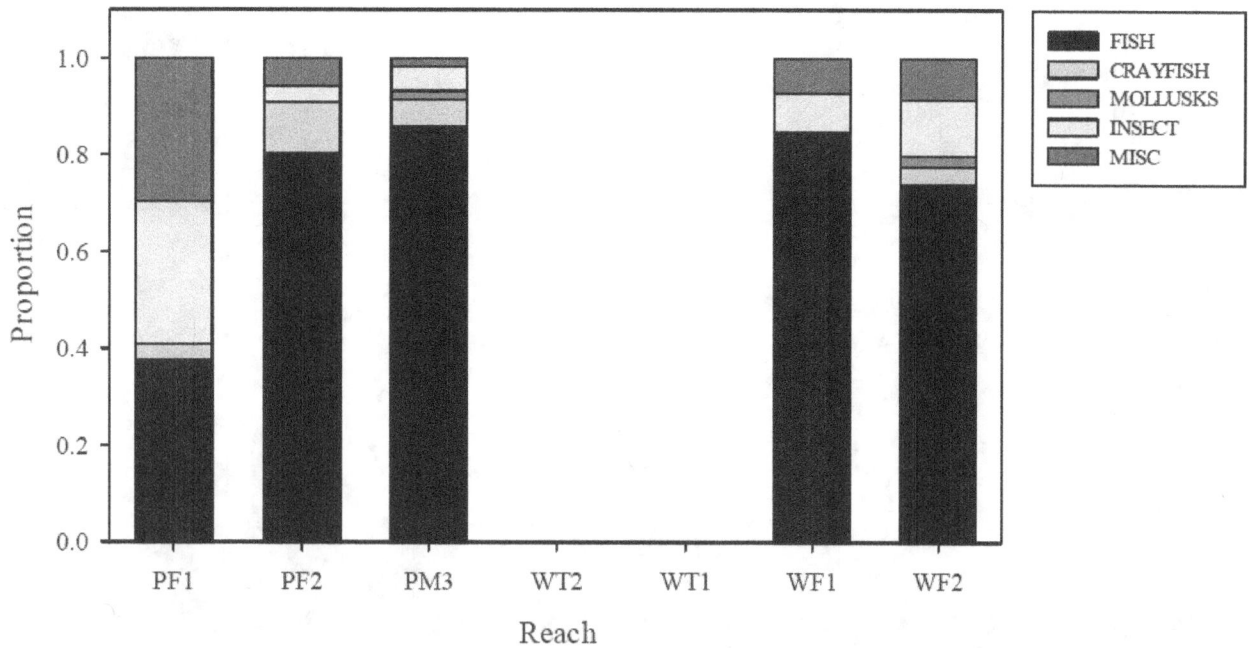

Figure 12. Diet composition by weight of smallmouth bass in 2011 (May 10–June 9), by reach in the Priest Rapids Project, Columbia River, Washington. Reaches with no column indicate no diet sample. Reach locations: PF1, Priest Rapids forebay near-BRZ (Boat Restricted Zone); PF2, Priest Rapids forebay; PM3, Priest Rapids mid-reservoir; WT2, Wanapum tailrace; WT1, Wanapum tailrace near-BRZ; WF1, Wanapum forebay near-BRZ; WF2, Wanapum forebay.

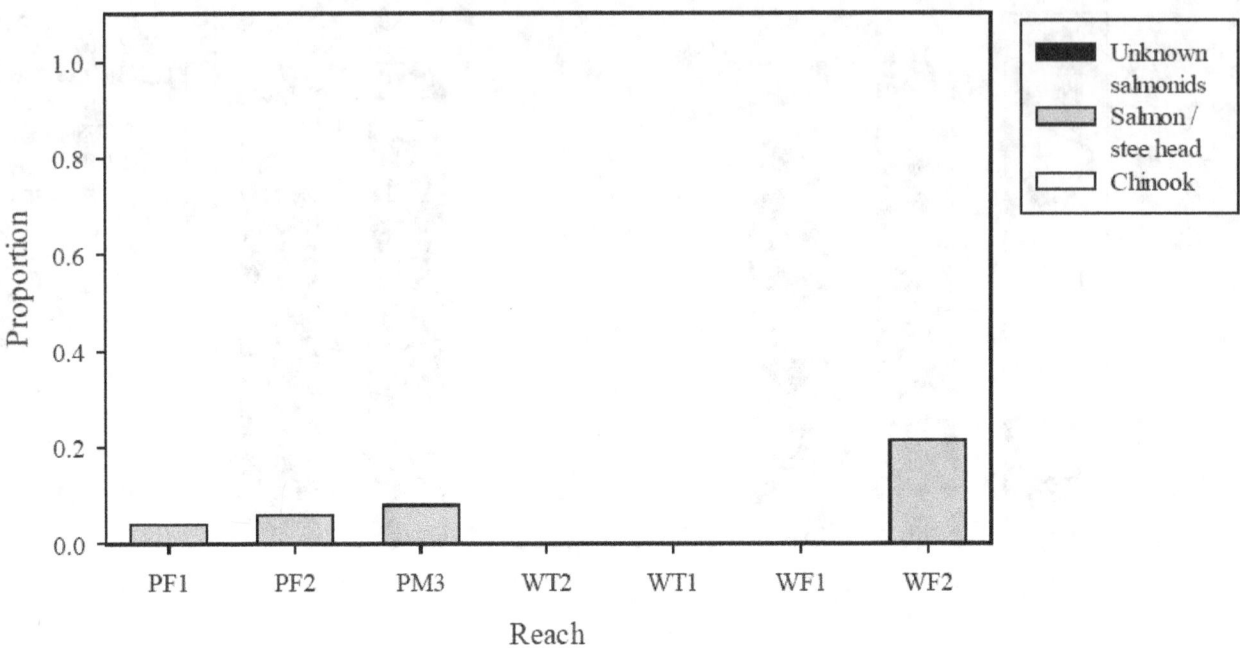

Figure 13. Proportion of fish in diet that are salmon and steelhead for smallmouth bass by reach in 2011 (May 10–June 9) in the Priest Rapids Project, Columbia River, Washington. Reaches with no column indicate no diet sample. Reach locations: PF1, Priest Rapids forebay near-BRZ(Boat Restricted Zone); PF2, Priest Rapids forebay; PM3, Priest Rapids mid-reservoir; WT2, Wanapum tailrace; WT1, Wanapum tailrace near-BRZ; WF1, Wanapum forebay near-BRZ; WF2, Wanapum forebay.

Table 1. Percentage of species composition by number of fish captured in the 2011 sampling season, Priest Rapids Project, Columbia River, Washington.

[Reach locations: PF1, Priest Rapids forebay near-BRZ (Boat Restricted Zone); PF2, Priest Rapids forebay; PM3, Priest Rapids mid-reservoir; WT2, Wanapum tailrace; WT1, Wanapum tailrace near-BRZ; WF1, Wanapum forebay near-BRZ; WF2, Wanapum forebay; Overall, all locations combined.]

Fish	Reach location							
	PF1	PF2	PM3	WT2	WT1	WF1	WF2	Overall
Bluegill	0.21	0.10	0.00	0.00	0.00	0.00	0.40	0.07
Bridgelip sucker	0.00	0.00	0.00	0.00	0.00	1.91	0.40	0.28
Chiselmouth	1.04	1.06	1.88	0.00	0.00	34.90	2.62	5.65
Sculpin species	11.02	1.92	1.77	0.20	0.00	2.21	20.32	4.19
Carp	0.21	0.00	0.21	1.02	0.00	0.00	0.80	0.26
Largemouth bass	0.42	0.00	0.00	0.00	0.00	0.00	0.00	0.04
Longnose dace	0.00	0.00	0.00	0.00	0.00	0.00	1.01	0.09
Longnose sucker	0.62	1.82	2.60	0.82	3.85	1.62	12.47	2.96
Lamprey	0.00	0.00	0.00	0.00	0.00	0.29	0.20	0.06
Largescale sucker	29.11	33.88	53.18	36.53	41.03	24.15	12.47	37.71
Northern pikeminnow	32.64	39.54	13.85	2.86	0.43	7.22	9.86	17.74
Peamouth	2.91	4.32	2.08	0.41	0.00	1.33	8.05	2.81
Pumpkinseed	0.21	0.10	0.00	0.00	0.00	0.00	0.00	0.04
Redside shiner	6.44	8.35	2.45	1.63	0.00	23.12	24.95	8.50
Sandroller	0.00	0.00	0.00	0.00	0.00	0.29	0.00	0.04
Speckled dace	0.00	0.00	0.00	0.00	0.00	0.15	0.20	0.04
Sucker species	0.62	1.73	16.04	53.47	51.28	0.29	1.21	13.46
Smallmouth bass	13.31	6.05	3.91	0.20	0.00	2.21	3.82	4.44
Tench	0.00	0.00	0.05	0.00	0.00	0.00	0.00	0.02
Threespine stickleback	1.25	0.67	0.16	0.20	0.43	0.29	0.60	0.43
Walleye	0.00	0.29	0.68	0.41	0.00	0.00	0.00	0.34
Whitefish	0.00	0.00	1.09	2.24	2.99	0.00	0.00	0.73
Yellow perch	0.00	0.19	0.05	0.00	0.00	0.00	0.60	0.11

Table 2. Summary of mean and standard error of catch per unit effort (catch per 10 minutes of electrofishing) for northern pikeminnow (total length greater than 170 mm) and smallmouth bass (total length greater than 150 mm), Priest Rapids Project,, Columbia River, Washington, May 2–June 7, 2009, May 4–June 2, 2010, and May 10–June 9, 2011.

[Standard error is shown in parentheses ( ). All efforts were randomly selected throughout the reaches except for "hotspot" (HS) analysis in 2011, which were stationary sites repeatedly sampled throughout the study dates. Reaches were combined in 2010 and 2011 to match reaches for 2009, with the exception of the mid-reservoir areas. An "*ns*" indicates the reach was not sampled. Reach locations: PT, Priest Rapids tailrace; PF, Priest Rapids forebay; PM1, Priest Rapids mid-reservoir, 2009; PM3, Priest Rapids mid-reservoir, 2010 and 2011; WT, Wanapum tailrace; WF, Wanapum forebay]

	Catch per 10 minutes							
	Northern pikeminnow				Smallmouth bass			
Reach	2009	2010	2011	2011 HS	2009	2010	2011	2011 HS
PT	0.013 (0.009)	0.082 (0.050)	*ns*	*ns*	0.0	0.0	*ns*	*ns*
PF	0.008 (0.003)	0.014 (0.007)	0.037 (0.005)	0.039 (0.007)	0.013 (0.011)	0.0	0.015 (0.003)	0.049 (0.022)
PM1	0.027 (0.008)	*ns*	*ns*	*ns*	0.014 (0.004)	*ns*	*ns*	*ns*
PM3	*ns*	0.017 (0.007)	0.044 (0.007)	0.042 (0.012)	*ns*	0.010 (0.010)	0.016 (0.006)	0.019 (0.008)
WT	0.004 (0.003)	0.005 (0.002)	0.007 (0.002)	0.005 (0.005)	0.0	0.0	0.0	0.005 (0.005)
WF	0.0	0.017 (0.008)	0.016 (0.003)	0.015 (0.006)	0.0	0.012 (0.006)	0.006 (0.002)	0.005 (0.002)

Table 3. Summary of northern pikeminnow diets analyzed in 2011 during electrofishing efforts by the Washington Department of Fish and Wildlife (WDFW) and by angling efforts by U.S. Department of Agriculture (USDA), Priest Rapids Project, Columbia River, Washington.

[Including thenumber of stomachs recorded as empty before (pre-maceration) and number and percentage ()after maceration (post-maceration), as well as the number and percentage () of non-empty, the number and percentage containing fish bones, and the number and percentage with no fish bones for the post-maceration stomach counts]

Collection	Pre-maceration			Post-maceration			
	Analyzed	Empty	Empty	Non-empty	Fish bones	No fish bones
WDFW Electrofishing	430	0	229 (53%)	201 (47%)	20 (10%)	181 (90%)
USDA Angling	131	0	50 (38%)	81 (62%)	76 (94%)	5 (6%)

Table 4. Summary of smallmouth bass (SMB), largemouth bass (LMB), and walleye (WAL) diets analyzed 2011, Priest Rapids Project, Columbia River, Washington.

[Including the number and percentage ( ) of stomachs that were empty, non-empty, or contained fish and the number of fish prey items (Fish Count) within the stomachs]

Species	Analyzed	Empty	Non-empty	Contained fish	Fish count
LMB	1	1 (100%)	-	-	-
SMB	202	38 (19%)	164 (81%)	131 (80%)	33 (20%)
WAL	18	6 (33%)	12 (67%)	11 (92%)	1 (8%)

Table 5. Results of visual diet inspection of piscivores in the field versus laboratory analysis (number of prey fish estimated).

[Prey categories: SH, steelhead; SAL/SH, salmon or steelhead; UNK/Other, fish unidentified]

	SH	SAL/SH	UNK/Other	Total
Field	1	14	130	145
Laboratory	1	27	259	387

Table 6. Summary of the mean consumption (Ci), abundance (Ai), and predation (Pi) indices, and standard errors ( ) for northern pikeminnow and smallmouth bass collected during randomized electrofishing efforts and site selected ("hotspot") efforts for reaches, Priest Rapids and Wanapum Reservoirs, Columbia River, Washington, 2011.

[Ci, mean consumption index; Ai, mean abundance index; Pi, mean predation index. Reach locations: PF1, Priest Rapids forebay near-BRZ (Boat Restricted Zone); PF2, Priest Rapids forebay; PM3, Priest Rapids mid-reservoir; WT2, Wanapum tailrace; WT1, Wanapum tailrace near-BRZ; WF1, Wanapum forebay near-BRZ; WF2, Wanapum forebay]

Reach	Northern pikeminnow			Northern pikeminnow Hotspot		
	Ci	*Ai*	*Pi*	*Ci*	*Ai*	*Pi*
PF1	0.177	0.248	0.068	0.123	0.301	0.035
	(0.116)	(0.062)	(0.044)	(0.123)	(0.045)	(0.035)
PF2	0	2.077	0	0	2.519	0
		(0.350)			(0.742)	
PM3	0.033	12.71	0.595	0.244	12.354	5.028
	(0.020)	(2.170)	(0.342)	(0.100)	(3.491)	(2.638)
WT2	0.153	1.109	1.191	0	0.624	0
	(0.153)	(0.386)	(0.191)		(0.624)	
WT1	0	0.047	0	0	0	0
		(0.047)				
WF1	0	0.246	0	0	0.131	0
		(0.045)			(0.049)	
WF2	0	0.918	0	0	0	0
		(0.225)				

Reach	Smallmouth bass			Smallmouth bass Hotspot		
	Ci	*Ai*	*Pi*	*Ci*	*Ai*	*Pi*
PF1	0.205	0.124	0.039	0.073	0.619	0.035
	(0.205)	(0.057)	(0.039)	(0.073)	(0.338)	(0.035)
PF2	0.167	0.797	0.157	0	1.260	0
	(0.090)	(0.214)	(0.087)		(0.252)	
PM3	0.334	4.627	1.827	0.179	5.572	1.493
	(0.259)	(1.854)	(0.991)	(0.158)	(2.332)	(1.023)
WT2	0	0	0	0	0.624	0
					(0.624)	
WT1	0	0	0	0	0	0
WF1	0	0.071	0	0	0.044	0
		(0.020)			(0.019)	
WF2	0.463	0.475	0.947	0	0	0
	(0.266)	(0.159)	(0.521)			

Table 7. Summary of mean predation indices (*Pi*) and standard errors for northern pikeminnow and smallmouth bass collected during May 2–June 7, 2009, May 4–June 2, 2010, and May 10–June 9, 2011, by randomized electrofishing efforts and site selection ("hotspot" = HS) efforts for reaches in Priest Rapids and Wanapum Reservoirs, Columbia River, Washington.

[Standard error is shown in parentheses ( ). A "*ns*" indicates the reach was not sampled. Reach locations: PT, Priest Rapids tailrace; PF, Priest Rapids forebay; PM1, Priest Rapids mid-reservoir, 2009; PM3, Priest Rapids mid-reservoir, 2010 and 2011; WT, Wanapum tailrace; WF, Wanapum forebay]

Reach	Northern pikeminnow *Pi*				Smallmouth bass *Pi*			
	2009	2010	2011	2011 HS	2009	2010	2011	2011 HS
PT	1.949 (1.817)	5.492 (3.306)	*ns*	*ns*	0	0	*ns*	*ns*
PF	0	0	0.110 (0.077)	0.132 (0.132)	0.172 (0.172)	0	0.200 (0.094)	0.109 (0.109)
PM1	0	*ns*	*ns*	*ns*	0.240 (0.240)	*ns*	*ns*	*ns*
PM3	*ns*	0	0.595 (0.342)	5.028 (2.638)	*ns*	2.221 (0.000)	1.827 (0.991)	1.493 (1.023)
WT	0	1.228 (0.811)	0.177 (0.177)	0	0	0	0	0
WF	0	0.251 (0.251)	0	0	0	0	0.645 (0.375)	0

www.ingramcontent.com/pod-product-compliance
Lightning Source LLC
Chambersburg PA
CBHW080348290526

45791CB00009BA/2786